IT
LAW

CYBER LAW
A view to Social Security

Anupa P Kumar

Cyber Law
A View to Social Security

Anupa P Kumar

July, 2009

3 Anupa P Kumar

Cyber Law

A View to Social Security

Anupa Kumar Patri

July, 2009

5   Anupa P Kumar

Cyber Law

A View to Social Security

Copyright © Anupa Kumar Patri, 1ˢᵗ July 2009

ISBN is 1449977863 and EAN-13 is 9781449977863.

This book is meant for educational purpose. The author of this book has taken all reasonable care to ensure that the content of this book do not violate any existing copyright or other intellectual property rights of any person in any manner whatsoever. In the event the author has been unable to track any copyright has been inadvertently infringed, please notify the author / publisher in writing for corrective action.

First Published 1ˢᵗ July 2009 by

Anupa Kumar Patri
Bangalore

Anup.patri@gmail.com

Acknowledgement

Cyber security standards are security standards which enable organizations to practice safe security techniques in order to minimize the number of successful cyber security attacks. These discussions provide general outlines as well as specific techniques for implementing cyber security. For certain specific standards, cyber security certification by an accredited body can be obtained. There are many advantages to obtaining certification including the ability to get cyber security insurance.

Throughout the pages of this book, you will see many examples, where businesses, governments and individuals are doing their respective parts to improve global security as well as adhering to the standard law & Cyber Law. You will also read about many areas in which security is still inefficient and in dire need of innovation. Indeed, there are many opportunities to get smarter about security.

The Global Innovation Outlook is designed to facilitate collaboration and openly share the many insights from its participants. But this report is only the beginning of the conversation and awareness to Cyber Law. I hope the essays in this report spark new ideas, in the Society for a better level of Security and mapping the same to the Cyber Law, going forward that endeavor to solve the world's most vexing security problems. The real work starts now.......

Anupa Kumar Patri

July, 2009

7 Anupa P Kumar

Table of Contents

Cyber Law…. A View to Social Security

Table of Reference

July, 2009

Anupa P Kumar

Abstract

Cyber Law or, less colloquially, Internet law, is a term that encapsulates the legal issues related to use of communicative, transactional, and distributive aspects of networked information devices and technologies. It is less a distinct field of law in the way that property or contract are, as it is a domain covering many areas of law and regulation. Some leading topics include intellectual property, privacy, freedom of expression, and jurisdiction.

It is one of the great paradoxes of the digital age. Tremendous advances in technology provide businesses, governments and individuals with an unprecedented capacity to ensure their safety and security. At the same time, the tools and methodologies available to disrupt society and to compromise assets have never been greater

So it comes as no surprise that security is an inconvenient but fundamental fact of life. Practicing good security takes time, discipline and money. Little wonder that securing the physical and digital assets of our clients, business partners and employees has been a significant part of our business for decades.

But providing security in this era of globalization takes more than one company, or even one government. Security in the 21st century requires a concerted, collaborative effort between businesses, governments and individual citizens. It requires that we push intelligence out to every edge of these networks, gather and analyze information in real time and react faster to all threats. In short, providing security today requires that we all get smarter.

Analytical Model of Cyber Law in Security & Society

Analytical approach which treats of the dogma or exposition of the abstract principles of law, as it exists, always has been a basic of formation of any code of law, which is dire need of society. Other approaches of philosophy of law like historical or ethical always lend a hand and assist to form a law but analytical approach provide basics to any law, as analytical approach always concern to basic principles, treatment of complex idea or concept, examine of the relation between the civil law and other forms of law, study of the legal sources of law, treatment of rights their kinds and classes and their creation and deal with legal liabilities etc.

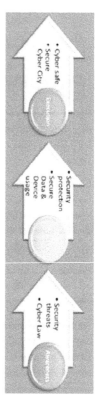

With the advent of digital telecommunication technology, computer and internet various kinds of issues and concerns are being faced by the man of today, these issues never ever been met hand-on by man in real world, before. The concerns relating to the computer and internet in fact are new phenomena of cyber space and in real world as well. The existence and form of things in cyber space may be different while the rights and liabilities may be the same.

The legal electronic realm is being developed, the rights and liabilities have to be fixed, legal electronic documents are being formed, jurisdiction and court venues are being determined and online ethics is being emphasized etc all these required a specific

July, 2009

philosophy of law to envelop all the issues and propositions of cyber space that would be cyber jurisprudence.

Legal issues relating to the electronic and internet in this contemporary world as being necessitated of new kind of jurisprudence. Cyber jurisprudence gives an analysis of the law where, is no land and even there is no border, where all things may be different from the physical world, they may be virtual from origin and nature.

Certain fundamental conceptions have to be grasped before the particular provision of law relating to them can be properly understood e.g. ownership, possession, jurisdiction, liability, rights etc in the realm of cyber space, these form subject of cyber jurisprudence. Without studying cyber jurisprudence, it will not be possible to understand any specific rules of cyber law. The cyber jurisprudence may therefore be described as 'the eye of cyber law'.

> "Society moves faster and is more complicated today than ever before. We expect access to communications and information anytime, anywhere, on any device. And security threats are constantly attempting to undermine these services. That's why it takes a monumental effort to secure the infrastructure

We may find virtual world with virtual rules and policies, along with the virtual subject matter, virtual contract, virtual disputes, virtual property, virtual possession and virtual court. Cyber jurisprudence deals with the composite idea of cyber jurisdiction and cyber court's venue in the cyberspace. It emphasis to recognize cyber uniform rules and policies at international level, it also discusses with the netizens and netiquates.

Security & Society.

Society owes its very existence to the basic human need for collective security. In this way, security and society are synonymous. Without one, the other ceases to be.

But the relationship between security and society has grown increasingly complex and dynamic over the last two decades. Never before has the balance between the two been more in flux, as globalization, interdependence and digital technologies have literally reshaped the foundations of society, challenging every accepted approach to its security.

Today, we are a truly global society, traveling freely and conducting business without borders over a communications network that connects virtually every person on the planet. The speed with which this change has taken hold has created unprecedented opportunity, both legitimate and otherwise. As business models and lifestyles have migrated from the physical world to the digital world, so too have criminal elements and other destabilizing forces.

It's all part of the inevitable security power struggle and the reason why truly complete security is not an attainable goal. Perhaps this is why many believe that security strategies should focus more on resiliency, or the ability to absorb and respond to attacks, rather than hardening perimeters and securing boundaries. Or that society needs to take a more distributed approach to security, empowering and enabling each of the world's security stakeholders to take more responsibility for the collective.

On the following pages, you will find a more detailed description of the concept of distributed security, as well as further insights culled from a series of six brainstorming sessions, or "deep dives," that IBM convened around the world in 2008. These meetings brought together business leaders, government officials, entrepreneurs, academics and nonprofits to ask the hard questions about the future of security.

The end result of this effort is not, of course, a solution to the world's security problems. This report is instead a collection of innovative security strategies for a globally connected world, strategies in which every government, business and citizen has a role to play.

Cyber Law Hypothesis

Issues of jurisdiction and sovereignty have quickly come to the fore in the era of the Internet. The Internet does not tend to make geographical and jurisdictional boundaries clear, but Internet users remain in physical jurisdictions and are subject to laws independent of their presence on the Internet. As such, a single transaction may involve the laws of at least three jurisdictions: 1) the laws of the state/nation in which the user resides, 2) the laws of the state/nation that apply where the server hosting the transaction is located, and 3) the laws of the state/nation which apply to the person or business with whom the transaction takes place. So a user in one of the United States conducting a transaction with another user in Britain through a server in Canada could theoretically be subject to the laws of all three countries as they relate to the transaction at hand.

Jurisdiction is an aspect of state sovereignty and it refers to judicial, legislative and administrative competence. Although jurisdiction is an aspect of sovereignty, it is not coextensive with it. The laws of a nation may have extraterritorial impact extending the jurisdiction beyond the sovereign and territorial limits of that nation. This is particularly problematic as the medium of the Internet does not explicitly recognize sovereignty and territorial limitations. There is no uniform, international jurisdictional law of universal application, and such questions are generally a matter of conflict of laws, particularly private international law. An example would be where the contents of a web site are legal in one country and illegal in another. In the absence of a uniform jurisdictional code, legal practitioners are generally left with a conflict of law issue.

Another major problem of cyberlaw lies in whether to treat the Internet as if it were physical space (and thus subject to a given jurisdiction's laws) or to act as if the Internet is a world unto itself (and therefore free of such restraints). Those who favor the latter view often feel that government should leave the Internet community to self-regulate. John Perry Barlow, for example, has addressed the governments of the world and stated, "Where there are real conflicts, where there are wrongs, we will identify them and address them by our means. We are forming our own Social Contract . This governance will arise according to the conditions of our world, not yours. Our world is different" (Barlow, A Declaration of the Independence of Cyberspace). A more balanced alternative is the Declaration of Cybersecession: "Human beings possess a mind, which they are absolutely free to inhabit with no legal constraints. Human civilization is developing its own (collective) mind. All we want is to be free to inhabit it with no legal constraints. Since you make sure we cannot harm you, you have no ethical right to intrude our lives. So stop intruding!" . Other scholars argue for more of a compromise between the two notions, such as Lawrence Lessig's argument that "The problem for law is to work out how the norms of the two communities are to apply given that the subject to whom they apply may be in both places at once" (Lessig, Code 190).

Though rhetorically attractive, cybersecession initiatives have had little real impact on the Internet or the laws governing it. In practical terms, a user of the Internet is subject to the laws of the state or nation within which he or she goes online. Thus, in the U.S., Jake Baker faced criminal charges for his e-conduct (see Free Speech), and numerous users of peer-to-peer file-sharing software were subject to civil lawsuits for copyright infringement. This system runs into conflicts, however, when these suits are international in nature. Simply put, legal conduct in one nation may be decidedly illegal in another. In fact, even different standards concerning the burden of proof in a civil case can cause jurisdictional problems. For example, an American celebrity, claiming to be insulted by an online American magazine, faces a difficult task of winning a lawsuit against that magazine for libel. But if the celebrity has ties, economic or otherwise, to England, he or she can sue for libel in the British court system, where the standard of "libelous speech" is far lower.

Internet regulation in other countries

While there is some United States law that does restrict access to materials on the internet, it does not truly filter the internet. Many Asian and Middle Eastern nations use any number of combinations of code-based regulation (one of Lessig's four methods of net regulation) to block material that their governments have deemed inappropriate for their citizens to view. China and Saudi Arabia are two excellent examples of nations that have achieved high degrees of success in regulating their citizens access to the internet (for further reading, please see ONI's studies on both: http://www.opennetinitiative.net/studies/saudi/ and http://www.opennetinitiative.net/studies/china/)

Pavan Duggal, Advocate, Supreme Court and Cyber law expert has also been vocal about India's Information Technology Act 2000, and did not find it adequate due to various flaws in it.[5] He has been critical of the efficacy of new Amendments to IT Act 2000 in India. He believes that new amendments,passed by Indian Parliament in Dec 2008, are not at all sufficient in the context of the emerging needs of India and there are various glaring loopholes

Law: Standard East Coast Code, and the most self-evident of the four modes of regulation. As the numerous statutes, evolving case law and precedents make clear, many actions on the internet are already subject to conventional legislation (both with regard to transactions conducted on the internet and images posted). Areas like gambling, child pornography, and fraud are regulated in very similar ways online as off-line. While one of the most controversial and unclear areas of evolving laws is the determination of what forum has subject matter jurisdiction over activity (economic and other) conducted on the internet, particularly as cross border transactions affect local jurisdictions, it is certainly clear that substantial portions of internet activity are subject to traditional regulation, and that conduct that is unlawful off-line is presumptively unlawful online, and subject to similar laws and regulations. Scandals with major corporations led to US legislation rethinking corporate governance regulations such as the Sarbanes-Oxley Act.

Architecture: West Coast Code: these mechanisms concern the parameters of how information can and cannot be transmitted across the internet. Everything from internet filtering software (which searches for keywords or specific URLs and blocks them before they can even appear on the computer requesting them), to encryption programs, to the very basic architecture of TCP/IP protocol, falls within this category of regulation. It is arguable that all other modes of regulation either rely on, or are significantly supported by, regulation via West Coast Code.

Norms: As in all other modes of social interaction, conduct is regulated by social norms and conventions in significant ways. While certain activities or kinds of conduct online may not be specifically prohibited by the code architecture of the internet, or expressly prohibited by applicable law, nevertheless these activities or conduct will be invisibly regulated by the inherent standards of the community, in this case the internet "users." And just as certain patterns of conduct will cause an individual to be ostracized from our real world society, so too certain actions will be censored or self-regulated by the norms of whatever community one chooses to associate with on the internet.

Markets: Closely allied with regulation by virtue of social norms, markets also regulate certain patterns of conduct on the internet. While economic markets will have limited influence over non-commercial portions of the internet, the internet also creates a virtual marketplace for information, and such information affects everything from the comparative valuation of services to the traditional valuation of stocks. In addition, the increase in popularity of the internet as a means for transacting all forms of commercial activity, and as a forum for advertisement, has brought the laws of supply and demand in cyberspace.

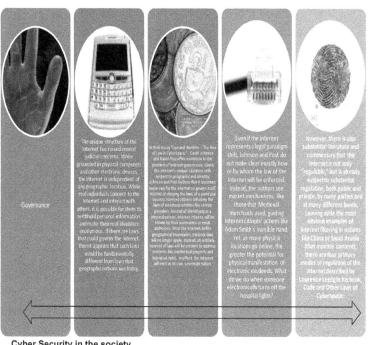

Governance

The unique structure of the internet has raised several judicial concerns. While grounded in physical computers and other electronic devices, the internet is independent of any geographic location. While real individuals connect to the internet and interact with others, it is possible for them to withhold personal information and make their real identities anonymous. If there are laws that could govern the internet, then it appears that such laws would be fundamentally different from laws that geographic nations use today.

In their essay "Law and Borders - The Rise of Law in Cyberspace," David Johnson and David Post offer a solution to the problem of internet governance. Given the internet's unique situation with respect to geography and identity, Johnson and Post believe that it becomes necessary for the internet to govern itself. Instead of obeying the laws of a particular country, internet citizens will obey the laws of electronic entities like service providers. Instead of identifying as a physical person, internet citizens will be known by their usernames or email addresses. Since the internet defies geographical boundaries, national laws will no longer apply. Instead, an entirely new set of laws will be created to address concerns like intellectual property and individual rights. In effect, the internet will exist as its own sovereign nation.

Even if the internet represents a legal paradigm shift, Johnson and Post do not make clear exactly how or by whom the law of the internet will be enforced. Instead, the authors see market mechanisms, like those that Medieval merchants used, guiding internet citizens' actions like Adam Smith's invisible hand. Yet, as more physical locations go online, the greater the potential for physical manifestation of electronic misdeeds. What do we do when someone electronically turns off the hospital lights?

However, there is also substantial literature and commentary that the internet is not only "regulable," but is already subject to substantial regulation, both public and private, by many parties and at many different levels. Leaving aside the most obvious examples of internet filtering in nations like China or Saudi Arabia (that monitor content), there are four primary modes of regulation of the internet described by Lawrence Lessig in his book Code and Other Laws of Cyberspace:

Cyber Security in the society

E-Governance

e-Government (short for electronic government, also known as e-gov, digital government,

online government or transformational government) is a diffused neologism used to refer

to the use of information and communication technology to provide and improve

government services, transactions and interactions with citizens, businesses, and other

arms of government.

UN e-Government Readiness Index

There are several international rankings of e-government maturity. The Eurostat

rankings, Economist, Brown University, and the UN e-Government Readiness Index are

among the most frequently cites. The United Nations conduct an annual e-Government

survey which includes a section titled e-Government Readiness. It is a comparative

ranking of the countries of the world according to two primary indicators:

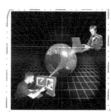

i) the state of e-government readiness; and

ii) the extent of e-participation.

Constructing a model for the measurement of digitized services, the Survey assesses the 191 member states of the UN according to a quantitative composite index of e-government readiness based on website assessment;

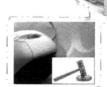

telecommunication infrastructure and human resource endowment.

The Next page is the list of the top 20 countries according to the UN's 2008 e-Government Readiness Index.

Security concerns are in some ways peripheral to normal business working, but serve to highlight just how important it is that your business users feel confident when using your IT systems. Security will probably always be high on the IT agenda simply because cyber criminals know that a successful attack is very profitable. This means they will always strive to find new ways

Rank	Country	Index
1	Sweden	0.9157
2	Denmark	0.9134
3	Norway	0.8921
4	United States	0.8644
5	Netherlands	0.8631
6	South Korea	0.8317
7	Canada	0.8172
8	Australia	0.8108
9	France	0.8038
10	United Kingdom	0.7872
11	Japan	0.7703
12	Switzerland	0.7626
13	Estonia	0.7600
14	Luxembourg	0.7512
15	Finland	0.7488
16	Austria	0.7428
17	Israel	0.7393
18	New Zealand	0.7392
19	Ireland	0.7296
20	Spain	0.7228

to circumvent your IT security, and you will consequently need to be continually vigilant. Whenever you need to make a decision about how to enhance your system, you need to have security uppermost among your requirements. When you are thinking about system security, there is no one aspect that will secure your systems - you need an overall security strategy.

It is no point having a network with a secure perimeter if the laptops of your business users are not security protected; the most secure email system in the world will not help if your business users send emails with confidential information because they are not security aware. Security has to be holistic, and you have to think about defending all aspects of your infrastructure - the servers and desktops, the network itself, wireless networks, computers that access your system remotely - all need to be equally secure.

You cannot eliminate security risks, but you can manage and mitigate the risk. The key to a successful security strategy is usually described as "Defence in Depth". The idea behind this is simple - you don't rely on a single protection for security, so that if one part of your security system is breached, the attackers only get as far as the next layer

Where the IT Act fails

The IT Act has many inherent limitations and shortcomings. The most significant one amongst them are:

The Act makes no reference to the protection of intellectual property like copyrights, patents or trademarks on the Net. It is also silent on domain-name infringement and cyber squatting. This seriously inhibits corporate bodies to invest in the IT infrastructure

It extends the application of its penal provisions to persons outside India, irrespective of their nationality if the offence under the Act relates to a computer located in India. Such extra-territorial jurisdiction is fraught with limitations as to its enforcement. Although, this seeks to afford protection for Indian cyber space from intruders from other countries but the example of Dawood and Quattrochi clearly bare

the ineffective enforcement machinery in India

It excludes property transactions to be carried out on-line due to the necessity of payment of stamp duty and registration of documents

The Act fails to address the issue of cross-border taxation that may arise in international contracts. The question of jurisdiction of a particular country over on-line transactions, which involves more than one jurisdiction, has also been left open

It does not deal with Internet privacy issues like prohibition of unsolicited commercial mail (spamming) and unauthorized use of private data collected on-line

It binds digital signatures to the asymmetric encryption system, limiting the scope of innovation in technology. This is a serious drawback especially since the technology is being replaced with a more secure system soon

It fails to cover control of cyber laundering of money, which can easily be used for criminal or terrorist activities especially given the situation post September 11.

Cyber Laws according to nasscom.org

Regulatory norms in Indian cyberspace

The arrival of the Internet and the World Wide Web made it possible for people to communicate and transact over cyber space. It was a revolutionary step for humanity, but it also created a significant need for the regulation and governance of these activities, a requirement that lead to the creation and implementation of cyber laws across the globe. India became the 12th nation in the world to adopt a cyber law regime during 2000.

The country's cyber laws are contained in the Information Technology, Act 2000. The Act came into effect following the clearance of the Information Technology Bill 2000 in May 2000 by both the houses of the Parliament. The Bill received the assent of the President Of India in August 2000 (IT Act 2000). The IT Act 2000 aims to provide the legal infrastructure for e-commerce in India. At this juncture, it is relevant to understand what the IT Act 2000 offers and its various perspective.

Chapter-II of the Act specifically stipulates that any subscriber may authenticate an electronic record by affixing his digital signature. It further states that any person can verify an electronic record by use of a public key of the subscriber.

Chapter-III of the Act details about Electronic Governance and provides inter alia amongst others that where any law provides that information or any other matter shall be in writing or in the typewritten or printed form, then, notwithstanding anything contained in such law, such requirement shall be deemed to have been satisfied if such information or matter is – rendered or made available in an electronic form; and accessible so as to be usable for a subsequent reference The said chapter also details the legal recognition of Digital Signatures.

Chapter-IV of the said Act gives a scheme for Regulation of Certifying Authorities. The Act envisages a Controller of Certifying Authorities who shall perform the function of exercising supervision over the activities of the Certifying Authorities as also laying down standards and conditions governing the Certifying Authorities as also specifying the various forms and content of Digital Signature Certificates. The Act recognizes the need for recognizing foreign Certifying Authorities and it further details the various provisions for the issue of license to issue Digital Signature Certificates.

Chapter-VII of the Act details about the scheme of things relating to Digital Signature Certificates. The duties of subscribers are also enshrined in the said Act.

Chapter-IX of the said Act talks about penalties and adjudication for various offences. The penalties for damage to computer, computer systems etc. has been fixed as damages by way of compensation not exceeding Rs. 1,00,00,000 to affected persons. The Act talks of appointment of any officers not below the rank of a Director to the Government of India or an equivalent officer of state government as an Adjudicating Officer who shall adjudicate whether any person has made a contravention of any of the provisions of the said Act or rules framed there under. The said Adjudicating Officer has been given the powers of a Civil Court.

Chapter-X of the Act talks of the establishment of the Cyber Regulations Appellate Tribunal, which shall be an appellate body where appeals against the orders passed by the Adjudicating Officers, shall be preferred.

Chapter-XI of the Act talks about various offences and the said offences shall be investigated only by a Police Officer not below the rank of the Deputy Superintendent of Police. These offences include tampering with computer source documents, publishing of information, which is obscene in electronic form, and hacking.

The Act also provides for the constitution of the Cyber Regulations Advisory Committee, which shall advice the government as regards any rules, or for any other purpose connected with the said act. The said Act also proposes to amend the Indian Penal Code, 1860, the Indian Evidence Act, 1872, The Bankers' Books Evidence Act, 1891, The Reserve Bank of India Act, 1934 to make them in tune with the provisions of the IT Act.

Advantages of Cyber Laws

The IT Act 2000 attempts to change outdated laws and provides ways to deal with cyber crimes. We need such laws so that people can perform purchase transactions over the Net through credit cards without fear of misuse. The Act offers the much-needed legal framework so that information is not denied legal effect, validity or enforceability, solely on the ground that it is in the form of electronic records.

In view of the growth in transactions and communications carried out through electronic records, the Act seeks to empower government departments to accept filing, creating and retention of official documents in the digital format. The Act has also proposed a legal framework for the authentication and origin of electronic records / communications through digital signature.

From the perspective of e-commerce in India, the IT Act 2000 and its provisions contain many positive aspects. Firstly, the implications of these provisions for the e-businesses would be that email would now be a valid and legal form of communication in our country that can be duly produced and approved in a court of law.

Companies shall now be able to carry out electronic commerce using the legal infrastructure provided by the Act.

Digital signatures have been given legal validity and sanction in the Act.

The Act throws open the doors for the entry of corporate companies in the business of being Certifying Authorities for issuing Digital Signatures Certificates.

The Act now allows Government to issue notification on the web thus heralding e-governance.

The Act enables the companies to file any form, application or any other document with any office, authority, body or agency owned or controlled by the appropriate Government in electronic form by means of such electronic form as may be prescribed by the appropriate Government.

The IT Act also addresses the important issues of security, which are so critical to the success of electronic transactions. The Act has given a legal definition to the concept of secure digital signatures that would be required to have been passed through a system of a security procedure, as stipulated by the Government at a later date.

Under the IT Act, 2000, it shall now be possible for corporates to have a statutory remedy in case if anyone breaks into their computer systems or network and causes damages or copies data. The remedy provided by the Act is in the form of monetary damages, not exceeding Rs. 1 crore.

Few Cases of Security

- NASSCOM, the premier trade body and "voice" of the IT software and services industry in association with Chandigarh Administration today inaugurated the state-of-the-art Regional Cyber Security and Research Centre (RCSRC) at Chandigarh. The lab was inaugurated by General S.F. Rodrigues, Administrator of Chandigarh and Governor of Punjab and Mr. Kiran Karnik, President, NASSCOM. NASSCOM will serve as a technical consultant for this initiative while the funding will be jointly provided by Department of Information Technology and Chandigarh Administration through Society for Promotion of Information Technology (SPIC), Chandigarh.

- RCSRC is the first cyber security research centre in the country that will engage a multidisciplinary team of researchers and faculty to conduct specialist research in the areas of information and cyber security and performance optimization in Networking in a cost effective manner. The team will conduct studies and

July, 2009

organise discussion platforms to educate and enable the students to prevent and handle the new age transgressions. The research work undertaken and data collected here will also serve as primary source of information for the entire cyber security focused research community.

Speaking at the launch, Mr. Kiran Karnik, President, NASSCOM, said, "Information security has been a key focus area for the Indian IT industry.

NASSCOM in association with various stakeholders like the union government, state administrations, academia, security professionals and the law enforcement has been taking steps that will ensure a strong security environment for Indian IT. We are very pleased to be associated with the inauguration of the Regional Cyber Security and Research Centre, and are hopeful that this will further raise the bar for India being at the forefront in identifying possible concern areas and spearheading new methods to curtail any security loopholes."

"Drawing on the strengths from Computer Science, Engineering & IT, the Center will serve as a valuable regional and national asset for the development of advanced security solutions, critical infrastructure protection, emergency readiness and response technology consolidating India's position with respect to information security", he added.

Elaborating on the need for RCSRC, General S.F. Rodrigues, Administrator, Chandigarh and Governor of Punjab, said, "Punjab with its encouraging policies is fast emerging as the most favored business and investment destination for IT and BPO companies. On this backdrop, it has become imperative for the Chandigarh administration to take the lead in research to create a technology rich environment conducive for constructive discussions and innovative ideas for further strengthening the security environment in the country".

The initiative is backed by the Board of Mentors that include prominent names from the IT industry, academia, defence services and Chandigarh administration such as Dr. Sundeep Oberoi, Principal Consultant, Information Security, TCS; Mr. Arun Seth, Chairman, British Telecom India; Dr. Bhaskaran Raman, Assistant Professor, IIT Kanpur; Professor Rudra Pratap, Associate Professor, Indian Institute of Sciences-Bangalore; Mr. Nandkumar Saravade, Director Cyber Security and Compliance, NASSCOM; Dr. Prem Chand, Executive Director, Tech Mahindra; and Major General D.V. Kalra, Chief Signal Officer, HQ, Western Command, Chandimandir.

CYBER LAW & INFORMATION TECHNOLOGY

Success in any field of human activity leads to crime that needs mechanisms to control it. Legal provisions should provide assurance to users, empowerment to law enforcement agencies and deterrence to criminals. The law is as stringent as its enforcement. Crime is no longer limited to space, time or a group of people. Cyber space creates moral, civil and criminal wrongs. It has now given a new way to express criminal tendencies. Back in 1990, less than 100,000 people were able to log on to the Internet worldwide. Now around 500 million people are hooked up to surf the net around the globe.

Until recently, many information technology (IT) professionals lacked awareness of and interest in the cyber crime phenomenon. In many cases, law enforcement officers have lacked the tools needed to tackle the problem; old laws didn't quite fit the crimes being committed, new laws hadn't quite caught up to the reality of what was happening, and there were few court precedents to look to for guidance. Furthermore, debates over privacy issues hampered the ability of enforcement agents to gather the evidence needed to prosecute these new cases. Finally, there was a certain amount of antipathy—or at the least, distrust— between the two most important players in any effective fight against cyber crime: law enforcement agencies and computer professionals. Yet close cooperation between the two is crucial if we are to control the cyber crime problem and make the Internet a safe "place" for its users.

Law enforcement personnel understand the criminal mindset and know the basics of gathering evidence and bringing offenders to justice. IT personnel understand computers and networks, how they work, and how to track down information on them. Each has half of the key to defeating the cyber criminal. IT professionals need good definitions of cybercrime in order to know when (and what) to report to police, but law enforcement agencies must have statutory definitions of specific crimes in order to charge a criminal with an offense. The first step in specifically defining individual cybercrimes is to sort all the acts that can be considered cybercrimes into organized categories.

United Nations' Definition of Cybercrime

Cybercrime spans not only state but national boundaries as well. Perhaps we should look to international organizations to provide a standard definition of the crime. At the Tenth United Nations Congress on the Prevention of Crime and Treatment of Offenders, in a workshop devoted to the issues of crimes related to computer networks, cybercrime was broken into two categories and defined thus:

a. Cybercrime in a narrow sense (computer crime): Any illegal behavior directed by means of electronic operations that targets the security of computer systems and the data processed by them.

b. Cybercrime in a broader sense (computer-related crime): Any illegal behavior committed by means of, or in relation to, a computer system or network, including such crimes as illegal possession [and] offering or distributing information by means of a computer system or network.

Of course, these definitions are complicated by the fact that an act may be illegal in one nation but not in another.

There are more concrete examples, including

i. Unauthorized access

ii. Damage to computer data or programs

iii. Computer sabotage

iv. Unauthorized interception of communications

v. Computer espionage

These definitions, although not completely definitive, do give us a good starting point—one that has some international recognition and agreement—for determining just what we mean by the term cybercrime.

In Indian law, cyber crime has to be voluntary and willful, an act or omission that adversely affects a person or property. The IT Act provides the backbone for e-commerce and India's approach has been to look at e-governance and e-commerce primarily from the promotional aspects looking at the vast opportunities and the need to sensitize the population to the possibilities of the information age. There is the need to take in to consideration the security aspects.

In the present global situation where cyber control mechanisms are important we need to push cyber laws. Cyber Crimes are a new class of crimes to India rapidly expanding due to extensive use of internet. Getting the right lead and making the right interpretation are very important in solving a cyber crime. The 7 stage continuum of a criminal case starts from perpetration to registration to reporting, investigation, prosecution, adjudication and execution. The system can not be stronger than the weakest link in the chain. In India, there are 30 million policemen to train apart from 12,000 strong Judiciary.

Police in India are trying to become cyber crime savvy and hiring people who are trained in the area. Many police stations in Delhi have computers which will be soon connected to the Head Quarters. Cyber Police Stations are functioning in major Cities all over the Country. The pace of the investigations can become faster; judicial sensitivity and knowledge need to improve. Focus needs to be on educating the police and district judiciary. IT Institutions can also play a role in this area. We need to sensitize our investigators and judges to the nuances of the system. National judicial Academy at Bhopal (MP) and State Judicial Academies are also running short-term Cyber Courses for Judges but much more is needed to be done.

Technology nuances are important in a spam infested environment where privacy can be compromised and individuals can be subjected to become a victim unsuspectingly. Most cyber criminals have a counter part in the real world. If loss of property or persons is caused the criminal is punishable under the IPC also. Since the law enforcement agencies find it is easier to handle it under the IPC, IT Act cases are not getting reported and when reported are not necessarily dealt with under the IT Act. A lengthy and intensive process of learning is required.

A whole series of initiatives of cyber forensics were undertaken and cyber law procedures resulted out of it. This is an area where learning takes place every day as we are all beginners in this area. We are looking for solutions faster than the problems can get invented. We need to move faster than the criminals.

The real issue is how to prevent cyber crime. For this, there is need to raise the probability of apprehension and conviction. India has a law on evidence that considers admissibility, authenticity, accuracy, and completeness to convince the judiciary. The challenge in cyber crime cases includes getting evidence that will stand scrutiny in a foreign court. For this India needs total international cooperation with specialised agencies of different countries. Police has to ensure that they have seized exactly what was there at the scene of crime, is the same that has been analysed and the report presented in court is based on this evidence. It has to maintain the chain of custody. The threat is not from the intelligence of criminals but from our ignorance and the will to fight it. The law is stricter now on producing evidence especially where electronic documents are concerned.

The computer is the target and the tool for the perpetration of crime. It is used for the communication of the criminal activity such as the injection of a virus/worm which can crash entire networks. The Information Technology (IT) Act, 2000, specifies the acts which have been made punishable. Since the primary objective of this Act is to create an enabling environment for commercial use of I.T., certain omissions and commissions of criminals while using computers have not been included. With the legal recognition of Electronic Records and the amendments made in the several sections of the IPC vide the IT Act, 2000, several offences having bearing on cyber-arena are also registered under the appropriate sections of the IPC.

As per the report of National Crime Records Bureau, in 2005, a total 179 cases were registered under IT Act 2000, of which about 50 percent (88 cases) were related to Obscene Publications / Transmission in electronic form, normally known as cyber pornography. 125 persons were arrested for committing such offences during 2005. There were 74 cases of Hacking of computer systems during the year wherein 41 persons were arrested. Out of the total (74) Hacking cases, those relating to Loss/Damage of computer resource/utility under Sec 66(1) of the IT Act were 44.6 percent (33 cases) whereas the cases related to Hacking under Section 66(2) of IT Act were 55.4 percent (41 cases). Tamil Nadu (15) and Delhi (4) registered maximum cases under Sec 66(1) of the IT Act out of total 33 such cases at the National level. Out of the total 41 cases relating to Hacking under Sec. 66(2), most of the cases (24 cases) were reported from Karnataka followed by Andhra Pradesh (9) and Maharashtra (8).

During the year, a total of 302 cases were registered under IPC Sections as compared to 279 such cases during 2004 thereby reporting an increase of 8.2 percent in 2005 over 2004. Gujarat reported maximum number of such cases, nearly 50.6 percent of total cases (153 out of 302) like in previous year 2004 followed by Andhra Pradesh 22.5 percent (68 cases). Out of total 302 cases registered under IPC, majority of the crimes fall under 2 categories viz. Criminal Breach of Trust or Fraud (186) and Counterfeiting of Currency/Stamps (59). Though, these offences fall under the traditional IPC crimes, the cases had the cyber tone wherein computer, Internet or its related aspects were present in the crime and hence they were categorised as Cyber Crimes under IPC. Out of the 53,625 cases reported under head Cheating during 2005, the Cyber Forgery (48 cases) accounted for 0.09

percent. The Cyber frauds (186) accounted for 1.4 percent out of the total Criminal Breach of Trust cases (13,572).

The Forgery (Cyber) cases were highest in Andhra Pradesh (28) followed by Punjab (12). The cases of Cyber Fraud were highest in Gujarat (118) followed by Punjab (28) and Andhra Pradesh (20). A total of 377 persons were arrested in the country for Cyber Crimes under IPC during 2005. Of these, 57.0 percent (215) of total such offenders (377) were taken into custody for offences under 'Criminal Breach of Trust/Fraud (Cyber)', 22.0 percent (83) for 'Counterfeiting of Currency/Stamps' and 18.8 percent (71) for offences under 'Cyber Forgery'. The States such as Gujarat (159), Andhra Pradesh (110), Chhattisgarh and Punjab (51 each) have reported higher arrests for Cyber Crimes registered under IPC. Bangalore (38), Chennai (20) and Delhi (10) cities have reported high incidence of such cases (68 out of 94 cases) accounting for more than half of the cases (72.3%) reported under IT Act, 2000. Surat city has reported the highest incidence (146 out of 163 cases) of cases reported under IPC sections accounting for more than 89.6 percent.

The latest statistics show that cybercrime is actually on the rise. However, it is true that in India, cybercrime is not reported too much about. Consequently there is a false sense of complacency that cybercrime does not exist and that society is safe from cybercrime. This is not the correct picture. The fact is that people in our country do not report cybercrimes for many reasons. Many do not want to face harassment by the police. There is also the fear of bad publicity in the media, which could hurt their reputation and standing in society. Also, it becomes extremely difficult to convince the police to register any cybercrime, because of lack of orientation and awareness about cybercrimes and their registration and handling by the police.

A recent survey indicates that for every 500 cybercrime incidents that take place, only 50 are reported to the police and out of that only one is actually registered. These figures indicate how difficult it is to convince the police to register a cybercrime. The establishment of cybercrime cells in different parts of the country was expected to boost cybercrime reporting and prosecution. However, these cells haven't quite kept up with expectations.

Netizens should not be under the impression that cybercrime is vanishing and they must realize that with each passing day, cyberspace becomes a more dangerous place to be in, where criminals roam freely to execute their criminals intentions encouraged by the so-called anonymity that internet provides.

The absolutely poor rate of cyber crime conviction in the country has also not helped the cause of regulating cybercrime. There has only been few cybercrime convictions in the whole country, which can be counted on fingers. We need to ensure that we have specialized procedures for prosecution of cybercrime cases so as to tackle them on a priority basis,. This is necessary so as to win the faith of the people in the ability of the system to tackle cybercrime. We must ensure that our system provides for stringent punishment of cybercrimes and cyber criminals so that the same acts as a deterrent for others.

Threat Perceptions

A survey released by the UK government has revealed that the British public is now more fearful of cybercrime than burglary and crimes against the person. According to its results, Internet users fear bankcard fraud the most (27 percent), followed by cybercrime (21 percent) and burglary (16 percent). This shows that hi-tech crime has firmly overtaken conventional burglaries, muggings and thefts in the list of the public's fears, as the Internet has become firmly embedded into the British society, with some 57 percent of households having online access. Interestingly, University of Abertay in Dundee, Scotland (UK) is now offering a BSc Hons in Ethical Hacking and Countermeasures.

About Regional Cyber Security and Research Centre (Rcsrc) at Chandigarh

- RCSRC is a security research centre setup at the Punjab Engineering College. The centre's mission will be to encourage, promote, facilitate, and execute interdisciplinary research in areas related to the nexus of the society and the digital world. The Centre will serve as a platform to:

- Aid and advise organizations in cyber security policy enforcements, conduct of security audits and incident handling

- Provide consultancy to various IT organizations and police departments on the secure design networks including deployment of security administration software like intrusion detection, management software for vulnerability checking, protection against port scanners, password crackers etc

- Educate and train manpower such as police, network users, IT professionals, and network security specialists in the cyber security policies and related skills so it is integrated as a part of their jobs.

- Facilitate research work for undergraduate and postgraduate students and researchers in the concerned areas

- Disseminate research results through journal and conference publications, technical reports, and public domain software.

- Create an online knowledge repository in the form of WEB/FTP server consisting of information in the above mentioned areas.

- Undertake projects with Government of India, NASSCOM, IT Industry in collaboration with academia.

- Conduct interdisciplinary training programs for state departments, IT industry and academia.

- RCSRC is a security research centre the primary focus of which is to conduct high quality research in the general areas of security, and performance optimization in Networking, at affordable costs. The Centre will be a platform to provide defense against threats such as information warfare. The Cyber Security Research Centre will carry out studies and hosts seminars that move society towards rational and informed discussion of these critical changes. Center's mission is to encourage, promote, facilitate, and execute interdisciplinary research in areas related to the nexus of society and the Internet. The research work to be undertaken in the Centre and data collected here shall be of great benefit to the entire Research community who shall be perusing the similar area.

- The technical consultancy will be provided by NASSCOM and the funding to the project will be by Department of Information Technology, Chandigarh Administration, which will be done through Society for Promotion of Information Technology (SPIC), Chandigarh.

- About NASSCOM's Ongoing Focus on Cyber Security Initiatives

- NASSCOM has been working closely with both the IT and ITES-BPO industry to create an Information Security culture, commensurate with world standards. One of the important aspects of NASSCOM's information security strategy is to strengthen the capacity of the Indian criminal justice system, including the police, prosecutors and judicial officers. The objective is to set up a robust framework to effectively investigate and prosecute cyber crime cases.

- As part of the Trusted Sourcing Initiative, NASSCOM has been working very closely with Indian law enforcement organizations to strengthen the capacity of the Indian criminal justice system, including the police, prosecutors and judicial officers. NASSCOM has spearheaded the following initiatives:

- Set-up cyber training labs in Mumbai and Thane for training police officers in cyber crime investigation. The Mumbai lab has provided training to 1039 police officers from March 2004 to February 2007. On the other hand, the Thane lab has trained 755 investigators from August 2005 to February 2007. The newly opened labs in Bangalore and Pune have trained 31 and 96 policemen respectively.

- In addition, approximately 574 police officers have also been trained through programs/ workshops conducted at Pune, Bangalore, Nasik, Jammu, Gurgaon, West Bengal, Aurangabad, Nagpur, Goa, Bhopal, Indore, Jaipur and Gujarat Helped Mumbai Police launch a toll free infoline with 24x7 call center Overall 2519 police officers and other personnel have been trained so far.

- NASSCOM is also generating awareness among consumers on cyber crimes through Cyber Safety Weeks. Cyber Safety Week is an annual event in Mumbai since 2003 and was also conducted in Hyderabad in 2006. It will be extended to more states in 2007

General security

- Choosing and Protecting Passwords

- Understanding Anti-Virus Software

- Understanding Firewalls

- Coordinating Virus and Spyware Defense

- Debunking Some Common Myths

- Good Security Habits

- Safeguarding Your Data

ings Keep You Safe Online

•Keeping Children Safe Online

Attacks and threats

•Dealing with Cyberbullies

•Understanding Hidden Threats: Corrupted Software Files

•Understanding Hidden Threats: Rootkits and Botnets

•Preventing and Responding to Identity Theft

•Recovering from Viruses, Worms, and Trojan Horses

•Recognizing and Avoiding Spyware

•Avoiding Social Engineering and Phishing Attacks

•Understanding Denial-of-Service Attacks

•Identifying Hoaxes and Urban Legends

•Avoiding the Pitfalls of Online Trading

Email and communication

•Understanding Your Computer: Email Clients

•Using Caution with Email Attachments

•Reducing Spam

•Benefits and Risks of Free Email Services

•Benefits of Blind Carbon Copy (BCC)

•Understanding Digital Signatures

•Using Instant Messaging and Chat Rooms Safely

•Staying Safe on Social Network Sites

Mobile devices

•Protecting Portable Devices: Physical Security

•Protecting Portable Devices: Data Security

•Using Caution with USB Drives

•Securing Wireless Networks

•Cybersecurity for Electronic Devices

•Defending Cell Phones and PDAs Against Attack

Privacy

•How Anonymous Are You?

•Protecting Your Privacy

•Understanding Encryption

•Effectively Erasing Files

•Supplementing Passwords

Safe browsing

•Understanding Your Computer: Web Browsers

•Evaluating Your Web Browser's Security Settings

•Shopping Safely Online

•Browsing Safely: Understanding Active Content and Cookies

•Understanding Web Site Certificates

•Understanding Internationalized Domain Names

•Understanding Bluetooth Technology

•Avoiding Copyright Infringement

Software and applications

•Understanding Patches

•Understanding Voice over Internet Protocol (VoIP)

•Risks of File-Sharing Technology

•Reviewing End-User License Agreements

•Understanding Your Computer: Operating Systems

Cyber Crime → An Overview of other cyber related offences.

Cyber Crime may be defined in a general way as an unlawful act wherein the computer is either a tool or a target or both.

Cyber Crime can be categorized as:-

General security
Attacks and threats
Email and communication
Mobile devices
Privacy
Safe browsing
Software and applications

Unauthorized access

Email bombing

Data diddling

Salami attack

Internet time theft

Logic bomb

Virus / **worm attack**

- Trojan attack
- Distributed denial of service attack

- Denial of Service attack
- Email spoofing
- Cyber pornography
- Intellectual Property Crime
- Cyber Stalking

DON'T LET THIS HAPPEN TO YOU!

Please think about what you would have felt if you were one of the 600 phone subscribers that were affected. Imagine what would have happened if there were an emergency with you - somebody was sick and you needed the ambulance.

You would stay out of harm - if you stopped for a moment to think - what if somebody hacked into your system or your program/opened your mail.

Though cybercrime statistics surveys are often distributed to system administrators inquiring about enterprises' annual computer crime experienced (that is, the methods employed by crackers, the frequency of system intrusions, the systems affected, and the dollar amounts lost because of the exploit or series of exploits) and the suspected identity of the crackers, these statistics need to be viewed with caution. One reason for caution is that often there are errors in the transmission of fact by the system administrators. Moreover, errors in reporting data may occur because no matter how honest the survey respondents try to be, a number of crimes go undetected and are therefore underreported by system administrators. Also, some system administrators may choose not to report known intrusions because of possible economic backlash for the enterprise, such as the loss of consumer confidence. In fact, the CSI/FBI annual survey findings indicate that even when intrusions are detected on system networks, only about 30% of these are ever reported to legal authorities.

Unauthorized access

Unauthorized access to computer systems or networks means any person who secures access or attempts to secure access to a protected system.

Email bombing

Email bombing refers to sending a large amount of emails to the victim resulting in the victim's email account (in case of an individual) or mail server (in case of a company or an email service provider) crashing.

Data diddling

This kind of an attack involves altering the raw data just before it is processed by a computer and then changing it back after the processing is completed.

Salami attack

This attack is used for the commission of financial crimes. The key here is to make the alteration so insignificant that in a single case it would go completely unnoticed, e.g. :a bank employee inserts a program into the bank's servers, that deducts a small amount of money (say Rs.5 a month) from the account of every customer. No single account holder will probably notice this unauthorized debit, but the bank employee will make a sizable amount of money every month.

Internet time theft

This connotes the usage by an unauthorized person of the Internet hours paid for by another person.

Logic bomb

This is event dependent program. This implies that this program is created to do something only when a certain event (known as a trigger event) occurs, e.g. some viruses may be termed logic bombs because they lie dormant all through the year and become active only on a particular date (like the Chernobyl virus).

Virus / worm attack

A View to Social Security

Virus is a program that attach itselves to a computer or a file and then circulate itselves to other files and to other computers on a network. They usually affect the data on a computer, either by altering or deleting it. Worms, unlike viruses do not need the host to attach themselves to. They merely make functional copies of themselves and do this repeatedly till they eat up all the available space on a computer's memory.

Trojan attack

A Trojan, the program is aptly called an unauthorized program which functions from inside what seems to be an authorized program, thereby concealing what it is actually doing.

Denial of service attack

This involves flooding a computer resource with more requests than it can handle. This causes the resource (e.g. a web server) to crash thereby denying authorized users the service offered by the resource.

Distributed denial of Service attack

This is a denial of service attack wherein the perpetrators are many and are geographically widespread. It is very difficult to control such attacks.

Cyber pornography

This would include pornographic websites; pornographic magazines produced using computers (to publish and print the material) and the Internet (to download and transmit pornographic pictures, photos, writings etc.)

Email spoofing

A spoofed email is one that appears to originate from one source but actually has been sent from another source.

Intellectual Property Crime

This includes software piracy, copyright. infringement, trademarks violations etc.

Cyber Stalking

The Oxford dictionary defines stalking as "pursuing stealthily". Cyber stalking involves following a person's movements across the Internet by posting messages (sometimes threatening) on the bulletin boards frequented by the victim, entering the chat-rooms frequented by the victim, constantly bombarding the victim with emails etc.

- **Security in Cyber Society Case studies**
- **Crackdown on Child Pornography »**
- **Security & Cyber-Crime**
- **December 15, 2007, Jerry Markon, Washington Post**

The spectre of child pornography, which was deemed to be under control in the early 90s, has once again reared its ugly head via the Internet. In the USA, this has prompted federal action with emphasis on identifying and prosecuting people deemed to be paedophiles or showing the propensity for molesting children. This programme, which has imprisoned people who have downloaded explicit images of children, has been denounced by its critics as excessive. Prosecuting child pornography is a sensitive area of operation and raises questions about the degree of punishment being proportional to the offence. However, society must resolve such issues in order to provide protection to our children, who are the most innocent and vulnerable members of the community.

- **The mouse that roared »**
- **Global Governance | Security & Cyber-Crime**
- **September 5, 2007, The Economist**
- This article talks about the ever increasing instances of cyber-attacks on vital cyber installations by different countries. What makes the nature of these attacks so serious is the fact that as more and more countries go online, the Internet is increasingly being used by governments for transacting work and business, and any attack on these vital installations can leave the country vulnerable and cut off

from the rest of the world. Specific instances of cyber attacks on a nation's infrastructure like the one by Russia on Estonia, have left that country completely paralysed, and although the Russian government claimed that it was the handiwork of certain disgruntled individuals, it was more or less established that the cyber-attack was conducted at the behest of the Kremlin. The latest incident of the alleged cyber-attack on the Pentagon by the Chinese government certainly clearly points the need for establishing a set of principles which govern the Internet and address such pressing issues.

- **Hackers take down the most wired country in Europe »**
- **Security & Cyber-Crime**
- **September 2007, Wired News**

This article details the recent attack on Estonian Internet by hackers allegedly at the behest of the Russian government. Estonia is a highly wired country, which means that it is always on the map of potential hackers and cyber terrorists. This article dwells on the intricacies on the two week episode and gives an in-depth analysis of the way the attacks occurred, as well as the measures taken by the administration to stem the tide of the attack. What happened in August when virtually all vital cyber installations were bombarded with large amounts of data, leading to suspension of Internet services for almost two weeks, was unprecedented and something which played out like a real war, albeit over the Internet.

- **India: Cyber cafes in cops' Net »**
- **Security & Cyber-Crime & IS Policies**
- **April 7, 2007, Mumbai Mirror**
- The Mumbai city police is planning to install a software to monitor all cyber cafes in the city and maintain a database of users. This primary aim of this move is to deter offenders who operate in cyber space. The manufacturers of the software envisage a server installed at the police headquarters, connected to the main server of every cyber cafe in the city, wherein, each time a user logs on to any computer in a cyber cafe, data including the user's name, address, identity proof, photograph, log-in and log-out time would automatically be transferred to the police server via the cafe's main server. The software is also capable recording

of the keys punched by a user while surfing the Net. While the police maintain that it could be a useful device to pinpoint offenders, the potential exists for this tool to also be used for surveillance purposes as well.

- **On 13.11.2001 the Cyber Crime Police Station at C.O.D.** arrested a Graduate Electronic Engineer working with a Multi National Company based in Bangalore, India for an offence under The Information Technology Act,2000. On 12.11.2001 Cyber Crime Police Station at C.O.D. Headquarters, Bangalore received a complaint from the above MNC that an unknown hacker having vested interest in closure of the above said organization has sent e-mails to their head office in US threatening either to close their operations in India or to face serious consequence. This e-mail was ignored by the US office but again the accused sent another e-mail warning them of serious consequences which was followed by downing of the Company's e-mail server in US. The accused again boasted through another e-mail of his enormous power and reach. The Bangalore office of the Company approached Cyber Crime Police Station at C.O.D Headquarters, Bangalore for investigation in this case. A case for above offence was registered on 12.11.2001 at Cyber Crime Police Station at C.O.D. Headquarters and investigation was taken up. During investigation police could identify the accused and could establish his links and modus operandi. On 13.11.2001 the accused was produced before the Honourable I Addl. C.M.M. Court, Bangalore and was remanded to Judicial Custody.

- **A young hacker found** a way to hack into a computer belonging to the phone company and that directs telephone traffic in the Boston area. After he got into the system, the hacker decided to reboot the computer, which basically made it crash. The first time he did this, the hacker completely shut off phone service for six hours to a regional airport so that the air traffic control tower had an extremely hard time communicating. The second time he crashed the computer, he cut off phone service to about 600 homes.

- The phone company reported this to the United States Secret Service, which investigated the case and identified all the kids involved. The Justice Department charged the ringleader of the group - a juvenile with several serious crimes. The student received very serious punishment: he lost his computer, had to pay $5000 to the telephone company, and work free in the community for 250 hours. He was also to be on probation for the next two years, and during that time he was not allowed to use any computer with a modem. That means, of course, he was off the Internet and all other networks.

Public worried by online ID theft

- The public are worried about credit card readers
- Concerns about identity theft are beginning to put people off shopping and banking online.
- In a survey commissioned by software firm Intervoice, 17% of people said they had stopped banking online while 13% had abandoned web shopping.
- Technologies such as online check-out services and credit card readers were pinpointed as potential ID risks.
- More than half thought that the government's proposed ID card was the best way to combat identity theft.
- Concerns about how secure identity is online have risen following high-profile phishing attacks.
- The term refers to the practice of creating look-alike websites, often of banks and other financial institutions, and duping people into visiting them and giving out personal information such as pin numbers and passwords.

Global security

- GlobalSecurity.org, launched in 2000, is a public policy organization whose mission is to be a reliable source of background information and developing news stories in the fields of defense, space, intelligence, WMD, and homeland security. Offering its information products through its website, the organization's editorial office is located in Alexandria, Virginia, USA. The current Senior Fellow on Homeland Security is Andrew Fois.

The website provides news and analysis on weapons systems and industry, comprehensive guides and directories of military and space related programs, entities, and facilities. GlobalSecurity.org also emphasises primary political documentation—legislation, political debates, hearings, and reports—materials that may or may not be available online elsewhere, but which GlobalSecurity.org states that it processes and collates to make more accessible to its readers.

- The website is freely accessible to readers

- and its income is based on online advertising.

- The website specifically targets "Subject Matter Experts",

- "Senior Leaders", "Junior Staff and Interns",

- "Concerned Citizens", and "News Reporters"; t

- he latter stated to be the site's most important

- online target audience

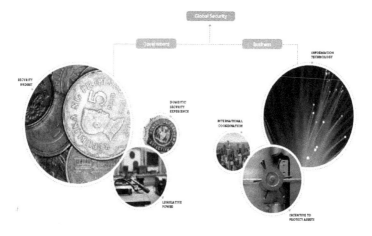

Anupa P Kumar

Security in Cyber Society Cyber Law in Security

A MILLION dollar question that may legitimately be raised is whether the cyber laws in India are good enough to protect Information and Communication Technology (ICT) assets in India? After some research at selective popular search engines, I came across this posting that seems to cover the topic in question very comprehensively. It reads:

"Cyber law in India is in its infancy and is struggling hard to meet the contemporary Information and Communication Technology (ICT) requirements. ICT Trends in India-2006, ICT Trends in India-2007, Cyber Security Trends by PTLB-2007, etc have proved that India has not paid enough attention to the legal framework for the information society and legal enablement of ICT systems in India. To worsen the situation we have a weak cyber and ICT security in India. Cyber and ICT security in India is an 'ignored world' and the same is not going to improve due to the faulty cyber security strategy of India.

This precarious situation has lead to an insufficient critical ICT infrastructure protection in India. The critical ICT infrastructure protection and management in India have still not got the attention of government of India and private industry players. In short, the ICT strategy of India needs rejuvenation so that we may have a sound cyber law and effective ICT and cyber security."

Now it seems to be very technical and an in depth research work but India is still lagging far behind when it come to cyber laws. Another aggravating factor that is marring Indian cyber laws is the lack of proper training to Indian police. The Indian police are totally clueless when it comes to cyber laws of India. There is a need to train the police, lawyers and judiciary for the proper enforcement of cyber laws in India.

The government of India must also take some effort to streamline Indian cyber laws so that the laws are strong. Although the government has proposed some amendments to the Information Technology Act, 2000 they have not yet become part of the law.

Proposed Cyber Law Requires Security Licensing

A View to Social Security

The Cybersecurity Act of 2009, known formally as Senate Bill 773, is best known for its radical recommendation to give the president authority to shut down parts of the Internet under cyberattack.

While well meaning, and a positive sign that the Obama administration is taking cybersecurity more seriously than his predecessor, some critics say it would activate not just an Internet kill-switch, but also a business kill-switch with burdensome licensing requirements for IT security professionals.

The issue is that businesses already struggling with resources to meet the current tangle of regulations -- SOX, HIPAA and PCI -- would have to add another to their project plans.

Section 7.a of the bill is short on details about the licensing requirement for the public sector, other than to say it would be administered by the Secretary of Commerce. It also isn't clear on whether it would be mandatory for cybersecurity professionals other than those working for the federal government.

Would a CISSP be enough for an IT security professional at private company? That remains to be seen.

Cyber laws in India

The centre must take some effort to streamline Indian cyber laws so that the laws are strong. Although the government has proposed some amendments to the Information Technology Act, 2000 they have not yet become part of the law..

General Law & Cyber Law a swift Analysis

Definition of law

Law is a system of rules, usually enforced through a set of institutions. It shapes politics, economics and society in numerous ways and serves as a primary social mediator in relations between people. Contract law regulates everything from buying a bus ticket to trading on derivatives markets. Property law defines rights and obligations related to the transfer and title of personal and real property. Trust law applies to assets held for investment and financial security, while tort law allows claims for compensation if a person's rights or property are harmed. If the harm is criminalised in penal code, criminal law offers means by which the state can prosecute the perpetrator. Constitutional law provides a framework for the creation of law, the protection of human rights and the election of political representatives. Administrative law is used to review the decisions of government agencies, while international law governs affairs between sovereign nation states in activities ranging from trade to environmental regulation or military action. Writing in 350 BC, the Greek philosopher Aristotle declared, "The rule of law is better than the rule of any individual."

Legal systems elaborate rights and responsibilities in a variety of ways. A general distinction can be made between civil law jurisdictions, which codify their laws, and common law systems, where judge made law is not consolidated. In some countries, religion still informs the law. Law provides a rich source of scholarly inquiry, such as legal history and philosophy, or social scientific perspectives such as economic analysis of law or the sociology of law. The study of law raises important and complex issues concerning equality, fairness, liberty and justice. In a typical democracy, the central institutions for interpreting and creating law are the three main branches of government, namely an impartial judiciary, a democratic legislature, and an accountable executive. To implement and enforce the law and provide services to the public, a government's bureaucracy, the military and police are vital. While all these organs of the state are creatures created and bound by law, an independent legal profession and a vibrant civil society inform and support their progress.

Few Law & Bare Act

•Banking Laws

•Consumer Laws

•Corporate Laws

•Criminal and Motor Accident Laws

•Direct Tax Laws

•Environment Laws

•Family Laws

•Foreign Exchange Laws

•Indirect Tax Laws

•Intellectual Property Laws

•Information Technology law

•Legal and Professional Laws

•Media Laws

•Miscellaneous Laws

•NRI Related Laws

•Property Laws

•Service and Labour Laws

•Cyber Law

Defining Cyber Law

Rapidly evolving area of civil and criminal law as applicable to the use of computers, and activities performed and transactions conducted over internet and other networks.

Cyber law or, less colloquially, Internet law, is a term that encapsulates the legal issues related to use of communicative, transactional, and distributive aspects of networked information devices and technologies. It is less a distinct field of law in the way that property or contract are, as it is a domain covering many areas of law and regulation.

Some leading topics include intellectual property, privacy, freedom of expression, and jurisdiction.

India became independent on 15th August, 1947. In the 49th year of Indian independence, Internet was commercially introduced in our country. The beginnings of Internet were extremely small and the growth of subscribers painfully slow. However as Internet has grown in our country, the need has been felt to enact the relevant Cyber laws which are necessary to regulate Internet in India. This need for cyberlaws was propelled by numerous factors.

Common Law

Considering the Internet is only a few decades old, it's not surprising that the security systems that guard this digital realm are less evolved than those that govern the physical world. In fact, many of the terms used to describe Internet security are still borrowed from the lexicon of physical security: firewalls, backdoors, patches and so on.

But for a medium as distributed and populist as the Internet, putting up walls hardly seems an appropriate response to the rapidly evolving security threats that plague it. That's why many GIO participants advocate the idea of community-based security, in which online groups that share a common interest police themselves, sensing and responding to threats as needed.

"Could there be a time in the future when bad behavior is punished by the community?" asks Pat Conley, Senior Vice President of Product Development at VeriSign. "On a very small scale you see this in forums and other online communities already, and this kind of self-imposed punishment is a way in which the community lays down the law."

For better or worse, the idea conjures up images of the puritanical village in Nathaniel Hawthorne's novel The Scarlet Letter. But these communities can take a variety of forms: a company; a political party; a social network. And in the digital world, communities are even more fluid and self-selecting. The only requirement is that the group share a common set of values.

Anupa P Kumar

Cyber Law Act in Different Countries

India

1. Information Technology Act, 2000

2. Karnataka Cyber Cafe Regulations

3. Gujarat Information technology Rules, 2004

4. .IN Domain Name Dispute Resolution Policy (INDRP)

5. Rules for Information Technology Act 2000

6. Semiconductor Integrated Circuits Layout Design Act 2000

7. Semiconductor Integrated Circuits Layout-Design Rules, 2001

8. .IN Domain Name Registration Policy

9. The Information Technology (Amendment) Bill, 2006

10. MOVED: Req: Indian Telegraph Rules, 1951

USA

1. THE DIGITAL MILLENNIUM COPYRIGHT ACT OF 1998

2. Deleting Online Predators Act of 2006

3. Adam Walsh Child Protection and Safety Act, 2006

4. CAN-SPAM Act 2003

5. FTC's Guidelines for Internet Advertising

6. Uniform Domain Name Dispute Resolution Policy

7. Computer Fraud and Abuse Act

A View to Social Security

8. Federal Trademark Act 1946 (The Lanham Act)

9. Children's Online Privacy Protection Act of 1998

10. Wire Fraud (18 USC §1343)

Europe

1. Data Protection Act, 1998

2. The Electronic Commerce (EC Directive) Regulations 2002

3. Regulation of Investigatory Powers Act 2000

4. European Model EDI Agreement Legal Provisions

5. UK Electronic Communications Act 2000

6. UK: Copyright and Rights in Databases Regulations

7. Council of Europe's Convention on Cybercrime 2001

8. The British Code of Advertising, Sales Promotion ...

9. UK: The Consumer Protection Regulations 2000

10. UK: NOMINET Dispute Resolution Service Policy (Ver. 2)

Malaysia

1. Digital Signature Act, 1997

Singapore

1. Electronic Transaction Act, 1998

Pakistan

1. Electronic Crimes Act 2004 (Sec 1 to 18)

2. Electronic Crimes Act 2004 (Sec 19 to 36)

Definition of Cybercrime

1. Cybercrime spans not only state but national boundaries as well. Perhaps we should look to international organizations to provide a standard definition of the crime. At the Tenth United Nations Congress on the Prevention of Crime and Treatment of Offenders, in a workshop devoted to the issues of crimes related to computer networks, cybercrime was broken into two categories and defined thus:

2. **a. Cybercrime** in a narrow sense (computer crime): Any illegal behavior directed by means of electronic operations that targets the security of computer systems and the data processed by them.

3. **b. Cybercrime** in a broader sense (computer-related crime): Any illegal behavior committed by means of, or in relation to, a computer system or network, including such crimes as illegal possession [and] offering or distributing information by means of a computer system or network.

4. Of course, these definitions are complicated by the fact that an act may be illegal in one nation but not in another.

5. There are more concrete examples, including the following items in the chart

Cyber crime report

As per the report of National Crime Records Bureau, in 2005, a total 179 cases were registered under IT Act 2000, of which about 50 percent (88 cases) were related to Obscene Publications / Transmission in electronic form, normally known as cyber pornography.

- 125 persons were arrested for committing such offences during 2005.

- There were 74 cases of Hacking of computer systems during the year wherein 41 persons were arrested.

- Out of the total (74) Hacking cases, those relating to Loss/Damage of computer resource/utility under Sec 66(1) of the IT Act were 44.6 percent (33 cases) whereas the cases related to Hacking under Section 66(2) of IT Act were 55.4 percent (41 cases).

  - Tamil Nadu (15)

  - Delhi (4) registered maximum cases under Sec 66(1) of the IT Act out of total 33 such cases at the National level.

- Out of the total 41 cases relating to Hacking under Sec. 66(2), most of the cases (24 cases) were reported from Karnataka followed by Andhra Pradesh (9) and Maharashtra (8).

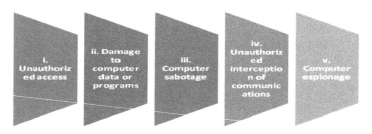

Advantages of Cyber Laws

The IT Act 2000 attempts to change outdated laws and provides ways to deal with cyber crimes. We need such laws so that people can perform purchase transactions over the Net through credit cards without fear of misuse. The Act offers the much-needed legal framework so that information is not denied legal effect, validity or enforceability, solely on the ground that it is in the form of electronic records.

In view of the growth in transactions and communications carried out through electronic records, the Act seeks to empower government departments to accept filing, creating and retention of official documents in the digital format. The Act has also proposed a

July, 2009

legal framework for the authentication and origin of electronic records / communications through digital signature.

> From the perspective of e-commerce in India, the IT Act 2000 and its provisions contain many positive aspects. Firstly, the implications of these provisions for the e-businesses would be that email would now be a valid and legal form of communication in our country that can be duly produced and approved in a court of law.

> Companies shall now be able to carry out electronic commerce using the legal infrastructure provided by the Act.

> Digital signatures have been given legal validity and sanction in the Act.

> The Act throws open the doors for the entry of corporate companies in the business of being Certifying Authorities for issuing Digital Signatures Certificates.

> The Act now allows Government to issue notification on the web thus heralding e-governance.

> The Act enables the companies to file any form, application or any other document with any office, authority, body or agency owned or controlled by the appropriate Government in electronic form by means of such electronic form as may be prescribed by the appropriate Government.

> The IT Act also addresses the important issues of security, which are so critical to the success of electronic transactions. The Act has given a legal definition to the concept of secure digital signatures that would be required to have been passed through a system of a security procedure, as stipulated by the Government at a later date.

> Under the IT Act, 2000, it shall now be possible for corporate to have a statutory remedy in case if anyone breaks into their computer systems or network and causes damages or copies data. The remedy provided by the Act is in the form of monetary damages, not exceeding Rs. 1 crore.

Anupa P Kumar

Cyber Law in INDIA

The information technology is a double edge sword, which can be used for destructive as well as constructive work. Thus, the fate of many ventures depends upon the benign or vice intentions, as the case may be, of the person dealing with and using the technology. For instance, a malicious intention forwarded in the form of hacking, data theft, virus attack, etc can bring only destructive results unless and until these methods have been used for checking the authenticity, safety and security of the technological device which has been primarily relied upon and trusted for providing the security to a particular organisation. For instance, the creator of the "Sasser worm" has been hired as a "security software programmer" by a German firm, so that he can make firewalls, which will stop suspected files from entering computer systems. [1] Thus, these methods may also be used for checking the authenticity, safety and security of one's technological device, which has been primarily relied upon and trusted for providing the security to a particular organisation. In fact, a society without protection in the form of "self help" cannot be visualised in the present electronic era. [2] Thus, we must concentrate upon securing our ICT and e-governance bases before we start encashing their benefits. The same can be effectively achieved if we give due importance to this fact while discussing, drafting and adopting policies decisions pertaining to ICT in general and e-governance in particular. The same is also important for an effective e-commerce base and an insecure and unsafe ICT base can be the biggest discouraging factor for a flourishing e-commerce business. The factors relevant for this situation are too numerous to be discussed in a single work. Thus, it would be better if we concentrate on each factor in a separate but coherent and holistic manner. The need of the hour is to set priority for a secure and safe electronic environment so that its benefits can be reaped to the maximum possible extent.

I. Cyber Forensics

The concepts of cyber security and cyber forensics are not only interrelated but also indispensably required for the success of each other. The former secures the ICT and e-governance base whereas the latter indicates the loopholes and limitations of the adopted measures to secure the base. The latter also becomes essential to punish the deviants so that a deterrent example can be set. There is, however, a problem regarding acquiring expertise in the latter aspect. This is so because though a computer can be secured even by a person with simple technical knowledge the ascertainment and preservation of the evidence is a tough task. For instance, one can install an anti-virus software, firewall, adjust security settings of the browser, etc but the same cannot be said about making a mirror copy of hard disk, extracting deleted files and documents, preserving logs of activities over internet, etc. Further one can understand the difficulty involved in the prosecution and presentation of a case before a court of law because it is very difficult to explain the evidence acquired to a not so techno savvy judge. The problem becomes more complicated in the absence of sufficient numbers of trained lawyers in this crucial field.

The Cyber Forensics has given new dimensions to the Criminal laws, especially the Evidence law. Electronic evidence and their collection and presentation have posed a challenge to the investigation agencies, prosecution agencies and judiciary. The scope of Cyber Forensics is no more confined to the investigation regime only but is expanding to other segments of justice administration system as well. The justice delivery system cannot afford to take the IT revolution lightly. The significance of cyber forensics emanates from this interface of justice delivery system with the Information Technology.

II. The need of Cyber Forensics

The growing use of IT has posed certain challenges before the justice delivery system that have to be met keeping in mind the contemporary IT revolution. The contemporary need of Cyber Forensics is essential for the following reasons:

(a) The traditional methods are inadequate: The law may be categorised as substantive and procedural. The substantive law fixes the liability whereas the procedural law provides the means and methods by which the substantive liability has to contended, analysed and proved. The procedural aspects providing for the guilt establishment

July, 2009

provisions were always there but their interface with the IT has almost created a deadlock in investigative and adjudicative mechanisms. The challenges posed by IT are peculiar to contemporary society and so must be their solution. The traditional procedural mechanisms, including forensic science methods, are neither applicable nor appropriate for this situation. Thus, "cyber forensics" is the need of the hour. India is the 12th country in the world that has its own "Cyber law" (IT Act, 2000). However, most of the people of India, including lawyers, judges, professors, etc, are not aware about its existence and use. The traditional forensic methods like finger impressions, DNA testing, blood and other tests, etc play a limited role in this arena.

(b) The changing face of crimes and criminals: The use of Internet has changed the entire platform of crime, criminal and their prosecution. This process involves crimes like hacking, pornography, privacy violations, spamming, phishing, pharming, identity theft, cyber terrorisms, etc. The modus operendi is different that makes it very difficult to trace the culprits. This is because of the anonymous nature of Internet. Besides, certain sites are available that provides sufficient technological measures to maintain secrecy. Similarly, various sites openly provide hacking and other tools to assist commission of various cyber crimes. The Internet is boundary less and that makes the investigation and punishment very difficult. These objects of criminal law will become a distant reality till we have cyber forensics to tackle them.

(c) The need of comparison: There is a dire need to compare the traditional crimes and criminals with the crimes and criminal in the IT environment. More specifically, the following must be the parameters of this comparison:

(a) Nature of the crime

(b) Manner/Methods of commission of the crime,

(c) Purpose of the crime,

(d) Players involves in these crimes, etc.

Thus, Cyber Forensics is required to be used by the following players of criminal justice system:

(a) Investigation machinery- Statutory as well as non-statutory

(b) Prosecution machinery, and

(c) Adjudication machinery- Judicial, quasi-judicial or administrative.

(d) Jurisdictional dilemma: The Internet is not subject to any territorial limits and none can claim any jurisdiction over a particular incidence. Thus, at times there is conflict of laws. The best way is to use the tool of Cyber Forensics as a "preventive measure" rather than using it for "curative purposes".

III. Conclusion

The growing use of ICT for administration of all the spheres of our daily life cannot be ignored. Further, we also cannot ignore the need to secure the ICT infrastructures used for meeting these social functions. The threat from "malware" is not only apparent but also very worrisome. There cannot be a single solution to counter such threats. We need a techno-legal "harmonised law". Neither pure law nor pure technology will be of any use. Firstly, a good combination of law and technology must be established and then an effort must be made to harmonise the laws of various countries keeping in mind common security standards. In the era of e-governance and e-commerce a lack of common security standards can create havoc for the global trade in goods and services. The tool of Cyber Forensics, which is not only preventive but also curative, can help a lot in establishing a much needed judicial administration system and security base.

Why Cyber law in India?

When Internet was developed, the founding fathers of Internet hardly had any inclination that Internet could transform itself into an all pervading revolution which could be misused for criminal activities and which required regulation. Today, there are many disturbing things happening in cyberspace. Due to the anonymous nature of the Internet, it is possible to engage into a variety of criminal activities with impunity and people with intelligence, have been grossly misusing this aspect of the Internet to perpetuate criminal activities in cyberspace. Hence the need for Cyber laws in India.

What is the importance of Cyber law?

Cyber law is important because it touches almost all aspects of transactions and activities on and concerning the Internet, the World Wide Web and Cyberspace. Initially it may seem that a Cyber law is a very technical field and that it does not have any bearing to most activities in Cyberspace. But the actual truth is that nothing could be further than the truth. Whether we realize it or not, every action and every reaction in Cyberspace has some legal and Cyber legal perspectives.

Does Cyber law concern me?

Yes, Cyber law does concern you. As the nature of Internet is changing and this new medium is being seen as the ultimate medium ever evolved in human history, every activity of yours in Cyberspace can and will have a Cyber legal perspective. From the time you register your Domain Name, to the time you set up your web site, to the time you promote your website, to the time when you send and receive emails , to the time you conduct electronic commerce transactions on the said site, at every point of time, there are various Cyber law issues involved. You may not be bothered about these issues today because you may feel that they are very distant from you and that they do not have an impact on your Cyber activities. But sooner or later, you will have to tighten your belts and take note of Cyber law for your own benefit.

Cyber law Awareness program

Are your electronic transactions legally binding and authentic? Are you verifying your customers' identities to prevent identity theft? Does your online terms and conditions have binding effect? Are you providing appropriate information and clear steps for forming and concluding your online transactions? How are you ensuring data protection and information security on your web site? Are you recognizing the rights of your data subjects?

Transacting on the Internet has wide legal implications as it alters the conventional methods of doing business. To build enduring relationships with your online customers the legal issues of e-transactions need to be addressed from the onset.

This Awareness view will cover

- ✓ the basics of Internet Security

- ✓ basic information on Indian Cyber Law

- ✓ Impact of technology aided crime

- ✓ Indian IT Act on covering the legal aspects of all Online Activities

- ✓ Types of Internet policies required for an Organization.

- ✓ Minimum hardware and software, security measures required in an organization to protect data

Both Sides of INDIAN Cyber Law or IT Act of INDIA

- ✓ Cyber laws are meant to set the definite pattern, some rules and guidelines that defined certain business activities going on through internet legal and certain illegal and hence punishable . The IT Act 2000, the cyber law of India , gives the legal framework so that information is not denied legal effect, validity or enforceability, solely on the ground that it is in the form of electronic records.

- ✓ One cannot regard government as complete failure in shielding numerous e-commerce activities on the firm basis of which this industry has got to its skies, but then the law cannot be regarded as free from ambiguities.

- ✓ MMS porn case in which the CEO of bazee.com(an Ebay Company) was arrested for allegedly selling the MMS clips involving school children on its website is the most apt example in this reference. Other cases where the law becomes hazy in its stand includes the case where the newspaper Mid-Daily published the pictures of the Indian actor kissing her boyfriend at the Bombay nightspot and the arrest of Krishan Kumar for illegally using the internet account of Col. (Retd.) J.S. Bajwa.

The IT Act 2000 attempts to change outdated laws and provides ways to deal with cyber crimes. Let's have an overview of the law where it takes a firm stand and has got successful in the reason for which it was framed.

- ✓ 1. The E-commerce industry carries out its business via transactions and communications done through electronic records . It thus becomes essential that such transactions be made legal . Keeping this point in the consideration, the IT Act 2000 empowers the government departments to accept filing, creating and retention of official documents in the digital format. The Act also puts forward the proposal for setting up the legal framework essential for the authentication and origin of electronic records / communications through digital signature.

- ✓ 2. The Act legalizes the e-mail and gives it the status of being valid form of carrying out communication in India . This implies that e-mails can be duly produced and approved in a court of law , thus can be a regarded as substantial document to carry out legal proceedings.

- ✓ 3. The act also talks about digital signatures and digital records . These have been also awarded the status of being legal and valid means that can form strong basis for launching litigation in a court of law. It invites the corporate companies in the business of being Certifying Authorities for issuing secure Digital Signatures Certificates.

- ✓ 4. The Act now allows Government to issue notification on the web thus heralding e-governance.

- ✓ 5. It eases the task of companies of the filing any form, application or document by laying down the guidelines to be submitted at any appropriate office, authority, body or agency owned or controlled by the government. This will help in saving costs, time and manpower for the corporates.

- ✓ 6. The act also provides statutory remedy to the coporates in case the crime against the accused for breaking into their computer systems or network and damaging and copying the data is proven. The remedy provided by the Act is in the form of monetary damages, not exceeding Rs. 1 crore($200,000).

- ✓ 7. Also the law sets up the Territorial Jurisdiction of the Adjudicating Officers for cyber crimes and the Cyber Regulations Appellate Tribunal.

- ✓ 8. The law has also laid guidelines for providing Internet Services on a license on a non-exclusive basis.

The IT Law 2000, though appears to be self sufficient, it takes mixed stand when it comes to many practical situations. It loses its certainty at many places like:

1. The law misses out completely the issue of Intellectual Property Rights, and makes no provisions whatsoever for copyrighting, trade marking or patenting of electronic information and data. The law even doesn't talk of the rights and liabilities of domain name holders , the first step of entering into the e-commerce.

2. The law even stays silent over the regulation of electronic payments gateway and segregates the negotiable instruments from the applicability of the IT Act , which may have major effect on the growth of e-commerce in India . It leads to make the banking and financial sectors irresolute in their stands .

3. The act empowers the Deputy Superintendent of Police to look up into the investigations and filling of charge sheet when any case related to cyber law is called. This approach is likely to result in misuse in the context of Corporate India as companies have public offices which would come within the ambit of "public place" under the Act. As a result, companies will not be able to escape potential harassment at the hands of the DSP.

4. Internet is a borderless medium ; it spreads to every corner of the world where life is possible and hence is the cyber criminal. Then how come is it possible to feel relaxed and secured once this law is enforced in the nation??

The Act initially was supposed to apply to crimes committed all over the world, but nobody knows how can this be achieved in practice , how to enforce it all over the world at the same time???

- ❖ The IT Act is silent on filming anyone's personal actions in public and then distributing it electronically. It holds ISPs (Internet Service Providers) responsible for third party data and information, unless contravention is committed without their knowledge or unless the ISP has undertaken due diligence to prevent the contravention.

- ❖ For example, many Delhi based newspapers advertise the massage parlors; and in few cases even show the 'therapeutic masseurs' hidden behind the mask, who actually are prostitutes. Delhi Police has been successful in busting out a few such rackets but then it is not sure of the action it can take…should it arrest the owners and editors of newspapers or wait for some new clauses in the Act to be added up?? Even the much hyped case of the arrest of Bajaj, the CEO of Bazee.com, was a consequence of this particular ambiguity of the law. One cannot expect an ISP to monitor what information their subscribers are sending out, all 24 hours a day.

Cyber law is a generic term, which denotes all aspects, issues and the legal consequences on the Internet, the World Wide Web and cyber space. India is the 12th nation in the world that has cyber legislation apart from countries like the US, Singapore, France, Malaysia and Japan .

But can the cyber laws of the country be regarded as sufficient and secure enough to provide a strong platform to the country's e-commerce industry for which they were meant?? India has failed to keep in pace with the world in this respect, and the consequence is not far enough from our sight; most of the big customers of India 's outsourcing company have started to re-think of carrying out their business in India .Bajaj's case has given the strongest blow in this respect and have broken India 's share in outsourcing market as a leader.

A View to Social Security

If India doesn't want to lose its position and wishes to stay as the world's leader forever in outsourcing market, it needs to take fast but intelligent steps to cover the glaring loopholes of the Act, or else the day is not far when the scenario of India ruling the world's outsourcing market will stay alive in the dreams only as it will be overtaken by its competitors.

Cyber Security & Benefits

Cyber Security & Threats

India lacks the expertise to deal with issues relating to the international affairs. Opening of the sector is likely to bring in foreign expertise that would build up capabilities in the services relating to foreign affairs.

Uncertainty about the Role of International Law Firms in India International law firms are allowed to function only as liaison offices, or foreign legal consultants.

The role of these firms need to be defined to avoid confusion over their status.

Setting-up of a Regulatory Framework for Foreign Legal Firms

A regulatory body overseeing the foreign companies functioning in India is highly needed. This body would lay the various restrictions governing the foreign law firms in India.

Slow Court System

The court system of obtaining justice is a very slow process. Foreign companies willing to enter the Indian market have to rethink as the slow process could impact their brand image.

Increasing Regional Competition Regional competitors like China, Korea etc are increasingly liberalizing their legal services sector .Indian government is concerned about this issue but has not yet made any formal decision on the liberalization of Indian legal services.

Cyber Security concerns are in some ways peripheral to normal business working, but serve to highlight just how important it is that business users feel confident when using IT systems. Security will probably always be high on the IT agenda simply because cyber criminals know that a successful attack is very profitable. This means they will always strive to find new ways to circumvent IT security, and users will consequently need to be continually vigilant. Whenever decisions need to be made about how to enhance a system, security will need to be held uppermost among its requirements.

Internet security professionals should be fluent in the four major aspects:

- *Penetration testing*

- *Intrusion Detection*

- *Incidence Response*

- *Legal / Audit Compliance*

The program attacks and the purposeful tampering to the database, repository and security systems are very common in these era. Some apparently useful programs also contain features with hidden malicious intent. Such programs are known as Malware, Viruses, Trojans, Worms, Spyware and Bots. Some of them are :

Malware is the most general name for any malicious software designed for example to infiltrate, spy on or damage a computer or other programmable device or system of sufficient complexity, such as a home or office computer system, network, mobile phone, PDA, automated device or robot.

Viruses are programs which are able to replicate their structure or effect by integrating themselves or references to themselves, etc into existing files or structures on a penetrated computer. They usually also have a malicious or humorous payload designed to threaten or modify the actions or data of the host device or system without consent. For example by deleting, corrupting or otherwise hiding information from its owner.

Trojans(Trojan Horsesare programs which may pretend to do one thing, but in reality steal information, alter it or cause other problems on a such as a computer or programmable device / system. Trojans can be hard to detect

Spyware includes programs that surreptitiously monitor keystrokes, or other activity on a computer system and report that information to others without consent.

Worms are programs which are able to replicate themselves over a (possibly extensive) computer network, and also perform malicious acts that may ultimately affect a whole society / economy.

Bots are program which take over and use the resources of a computer system over a network without consent, and communicate those results to others who may control the Bots.

Buffer overflow attacks

A buffer overflow is an attack that could be used by a hacker to get full system access through various methods. It is similar to "Brute Forcing" a computer in that it sends an immense attack to the victim computer until it cracks. Most internet security solutions today lack sufficient protection against these types of attacks.

As information technology continues to grow in scope and importance, it's impossible to overstate the value of managing the security of mission-critical computer systems that run an organization's most sensitive processes and functions. With security as one of their highest priorities, executives are searching for effective techniques to deliver maximum security while simplifying security management. In this regard, it's essential to develop forward-looking strategies to build and manage effective security programs that address both technical and management issues, since you can't achieve long-term security without dealing with both.

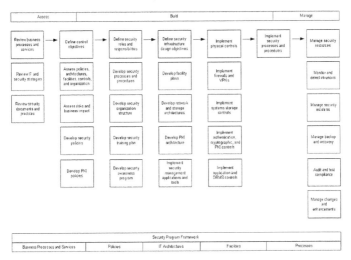

Security Assess, Build, Manage Model

Security professionals are living in a world in which they must deal with many different products from many different sources, deploying and managing them efficiently. Options for implementing security technologies can be overwhelming: scanners, intrusion-detection systems, firewalls, access controls, virus protection, VPNs, Public Key Infrastructure (PKI) systems, DBMS access mechanisms, and others.

Secure computing systems can run on a variety of platforms including UNIX, Linux, OS/400, Mac OS, Windows, OS/390, NetWare, Palm, Java-based devices, and many other alternative platforms. These may be connected through Ethernet, Fast Ethernet, Gigabit Ethernet, ATM, ISDN, frame relay, xDSL, and many others. Each set of security technologies presents unique deployment, management, and availability challenges.

How is the Security in the Cyber society Now

Cyber law act in India

The centre must take some effort to streamline Indian cyber laws so that the laws are strong. Although the government has proposed some amendments to the Information Technology Act, 2000 they have not yet become part of the law..

Government to sniff your emails

The recent terror attacks in various parts of the country during which terrorists allegedly hacked into wireless networks to send emails warning of imminent attacks has prompted the central government to consider monitoring e-mails on a full time basis. For this, the government has decided to install specialized software to check the content of e-mails which flow over four or five major ISPs.

Govt. may keep an eye on emails from abroad

According to , The Economic Times ,The Internet has thrown up new challenges to the government in terms of information security. The recent acts of defacement of websites as well as intrusions via the web has led to steps by the Department of Information Technology in India. These include a proposal to scan emails coming to India from abroad as well as setting up secure infrastructure for the hosting of government websites.

Government may soon find BlackBerry solution

This news report talks about the recent developments in the controversy over monitoring Blackberry traffic in India. It started when the Canadian company Research in Motion (RIM) that owns Blackberry services in India, refused to share the decryption code with the Department of Telecommunications (DoT). This had raised security concerns since the security agencies could not monitor the data that were being sent due to the high encryption codes.

IP address can mislead in online crime

This news item reports the sad case of a software professional who was wrongly convicted on charges that he uploaded offensive pictures of Shivaji on Orkut. The mistake, it is assumed, was done by making incorrect inferences on the IP addresses given to the police during investigation by the Internet Service Provider (ISP).

Online? Beware, you are under watch

Online crime is on the rise, not only affecting developed nations but also increasingly becoming a problem in developing countries. Many Indian netizens, especially those in the young population, are unaware of the risks of being online, even though more users are becoming targets without knowing it. The article warns of the dangers of online crime, which affects everyone from teens on social networking sites to consumers and businesses carrying out e-commerce transactions.

India ranks 14th in phishing attacks

The article reviews the proceedings of the recent Internet & Mobile Association of India (IAMAI) workshop which analyzed the major issues regarding the degree of control that should be exercised on the Internet. Cyber crime has assumed significant proportions in India as exemplified by the fact that India is now a major target for phishing attacks. om hackers in recent years.

How is the Security in the Cyber society Now

THE INFORMATION TECHNOLOGY ACT, 2000

An Act to provide legal recognition for transactions carried out by means of electronic data interchange and other means of electronic communication, commonly referred to as "Electronic Commerce", which involve the use of alternatives to paper-based methods of communication and storage of information, to facilitate electronic filing of documents with the Government agencies and further to amend the Indian Penal Code, the Indian Evidence Act, 1872, the Bankers' Books Evidence Act, 1891 and the Reserve Bank of India Act, 1934 and for matters connected therewith or incidental thereto.

WHEREAS the General Assembly of the United Nations by resolution A/RES/51/162, dated the 30th January, 1997 has adopted the Model Law on Electronic Commerce adopted by the United Nations Commission on International Trade Law; AND WHEREAS the said resolution recommends, inter alia, that all States give favorable consideration to the said Model Law when they enact or revise their laws, in view of the need for uniformity of the law applicable to alternatives to paper-based methods of communication and storage of information; AND WHEREAS it is considered necessary to give effect to the said resolution and to promote efficient delivery of Government services by means of reliable electronic records;

In this Act, unless the context otherwise requires,
(a)"access" with its grammatical variations and cognate expressions means gaining entry into, instructing or communicating with the logical, arithmetical, or memory function resources of a computer, computer system or computer network;

(b)"addressee" means a person who is intended by the originator to receive the electronic record but does not include any intermediary;

(c)"adjudicating officer" means an adjudicating officer appointed under subsection (1) of section 46;

(d)"affixing digital signature" with its grammatical variations and cognate expressions means adoption of any methodology or procedure by a person for the purpose of authenticating an electronic record by means of digital signature;

(e)"appropriate Government" means as respects any matter,-

(i) enumerated in List II of the Seventh Schedule to the   Constitution;

(ii) relating to any State law enacted under List III of the   Seventh Schedule to the Constitution, the State Government and in any other case, the Central Government;

(f) "asymmetric cryptosystem" means a system of a secure key pair consisting of a private key for creating a digital signature and a public key to verify the digital signature;

(g) "Certifying Authority" means a person who has been granted a license to issue a Digital Signature Certificate under section 24;

(h) "certification practice statement" means a statement issued by a Certifying Authority to specify the practices that the Certifying Authority employs in issuing Digital Signature Certificates;

(i) "computer" means any electronic magnetic, optical or other high-speed data processing device or system which performs logical, arithmetic, and memory functions by manipulations of electronic, magnetic or optical impulses, and includes all input, output, processing, storage, computer software, or communication facilities which are connected or related to the computer in a computer system or computer network;

(j) "computer network" means the interconnection of one or more computers through-

　(i) the use of satellite, microwave, terrestrial line or other communication media; and

　(ii) terminals or a complex consisting of two or more interconnected computers whether or not the interconnection is continuously maintained;

as a reference to the corresponding law or the relevant provision of the corresponding law, if any, in force in that area.

(k) "computer resource" means computer, computer system, computer network, data, computer database or software;

(l) "computer system" means a device or collection of devices, including input and output support devices and excluding calculators which are not

programmable and capable of being used in conjunction with external files, which contain computer programmers, electronic instructions, input data and output data, that performs logic, arithmetic, data storage and retrieval, communication control and other functions;

(m) "Controller" means the Controller of Certifying Authorities appointed under sub-section (l) of section 17;

(n) "Cyber Appellate Tribunal" means the Cyber Regulations Appellate Tribunal established under sub-section (1) of section 48;

(o) "data" means a representation of information, knowledge, facts, concepts or instructions which are being prepared or have been prepared in a formalised manner, and is intended to be processed, is being processed or has been processed in a computer system or computer network, and may be in any form (including computer printouts magnetic or optical storage media, punched cards, punched tapes) or stored internally in the memory of the computer;

(p) "digital signature" means authentication of any electronic record by a subscriber by means of an electronic method or procedure in accordance with the provisions of section 3;

(q) "Digital Signature Certificate" means a Digital Signature Certificate issued under sub-section (4) of section 35;

(r) "electronic form" with reference to information means any information generated, sent, received or stored in media, magnetic, optical, computer memory, micro film, computer generated micro fiche or similar device;

(s) "Electronic Gazette" means official Gazette published in the electronic form;

(t) "electronic record" means data, record or data generated, image or sound stored, received or sent in an electronic form or micro film or computer generated micro fiche;

the State Government and in any other case, the Central Government;

(f) "asymmetric cryptosystem" means a system of a secure key pair consisting of a private key for creating a digital signature and a public key to verify the digital signature;

(g) "Certifying Authority" means a person who has been granted a license to issue a Digital Signature Certificate under section 24;

(h) "certification practice statement" means a statement issued by a Certifying Authority to specify the practices that the Certifying Authority employs in issuing Digital Signature Certificates;

(i) "computer" means any electronic magnetic, optical or other high-speed data processing device or system which performs logical, arithmetic, and memory functions by manipulations of electronic, magnetic or optical impulses, and includes all input, output, processing, storage, computer software, or communication facilities which are connected or related to the computer in a computer system or computer network;

(j) "computer network" means the interconnection of one or more computers through-

(i) the use of satellite, microwave, terrestrial line or other communication media; and

(ii) terminals or a complex consisting of two or more interconnected computers whether or not the interconnection is continuously maintained;

as a reference to the corresponding law or the relevant provision of the corresponding law, if any, in force in that area.

(k) "computer resource" means computer, computer system, computer network, data, computer database or software;

(l) "computer system" means a device or collection of devices, including input and output support devices and excluding calculators which are not programmable and capable of being used in conjunction with external files, which contain computer programmers, electronic instructions, input data and output data, that performs logic, arithmetic, data storage and retrieval, communication control and other functions;

(m) "Controller" means the Controller of Certifying Authorities appointed under sub-section (l) of section 17;

(n) "Cyber Appellate Tribunal" means the Cyber Regulations Appellate Tribunal established under sub-section (1) of section 48;

(o) "data" means a representation of information, knowledge, facts, concepts or instructions which are being prepared or have been prepared in a formalised manner, and is intended to be processed, is being processed or has been processed in a computer system or computer network, and may be in any form (including computer printouts magnetic or optical storage media, punched cards, punched tapes) or stored internally in the memory of the computer;

(p) "digital signature" means authentication of any electronic record by a subscriber by means of an electronic method or procedure in accordance with the provisions of section 3;

(q) "Digital Signature Certificate" means a Digital Signature Certificate issued under sub-section (4) of section 35;

(r) "electronic form" with reference to information means any information generated, sent, received or stored in media, magnetic, optical, computer memory, micro film, computer generated micro fiche or similar device;

(s) "Electronic Gazette" means official Gazette published in the electronic form;

(t) "electronic record" means data, record or data generated, image or sound stored, received or sent in an electronic form or micro film or computer generated micro fiche;

(u) "function", in relation to a computer, includes logic, control, arithmetical process, deletion, storage and retrieval and communication or telecommunication from or within a computer;

(v) "information" includes data, text, images, sound, voice, codes, computer programes, software and database or micro film or computer generated micro fiche.

(w) "intermediary" with respect to any particular electronic message means any person who on behalf of another person receives, stores or transmits that message or provides any service with respect to that message;

to the corresponding law or the relevant provision of the corresponding law, if any, in force in that area.

(x) "key pair", in an asymmetric cryptosystem, means a private key and its mathematically related public key, which are so related that the public key can verify a digital signature created by the private key;

(y) "law" includes any Act of Parliament or of a State Legislature, Ordinances promulgated by the President or a Governor, as the case may be, Regulations made by the President under article 240, Bills enacted as President's Act under sub-clause (a) of clause (1) of article 357 of the Constitution and includes rules, regulations, bye-laws and orders Issued or made there undor;

(z) "license" means a license granted to a Certifying Authority under section 24;

(za) "originator" means a person who sends, generates, stores or transmits any electronic message or causes any electronic

message to be sent, generated, stored or transmitted to any other person but does not include an intermediary;

(zb) "prescribed" means prescribed by rules made under this Act;

(zc) "private key" means the key of a key pair used to create a digital signature;

(zd) "public key" means the key of a key pair used to verify a digital signature and listed in the Digital Signature Certificate;

(ze) "secure system" means computer hardware, software, and procedure that-

    (a) are reasonably secure from unauthorized access and misuse;

    (b) provide a reasonable level of reliability and correct operation;

    (c) are reasonably suited to performing the intended functions; and

    (d) adhere to generally accepted security procedures;

(zf) "security procedure" means the security procedure prescribed under section 16 by the Central Government;

(zg) "subscriber" means a person in whose name the Digital Signature Certificate is issued;

(zh) "verify" in relation to a digital signature, electronic record or public key, with its grammatical variations and cognate expressions means to determine whether-

    (a) the initial electronic record was affixed with the digital signature by the use of private key corresponding to the public key of the subscriber;

    (b) the initial electronic record is retained intact or has been altered since such electronic record was so affixed with the digital signature.

Any reference in this Act to any enactment or any provision thereof shall, in relation to an area in which such enactment or such provision is not in force, be construed as a reference to the corresponding law or the relevant provision of the corresponding law, if any, in force in that area.

Screening for dangerous blogs, sites

The Indian Central Government is putting in place an advance screening system at the country's international bandwidth

landing stations to block individual websites and blogs perceived as threats to national security. The technology to be put in place at the eight landing stations will be capable of blocking websites at a sub-domain level, thus saving internet service providers (ISPs) from a sweeping shutdown.

Computer hacking and cyber terrorism: the real threats in the new millennium?

As the new millennium approaches, we are living in a society that is increasingly dependent upon information technology. However, whilst technology can deliver a number of benefits, it also introduces new vulnerabilities that can be exploited by persons with the necessary technical skills. Hackers represent a well-known threat in this respect and are responsible for a significant degree of disruption and damage to information systems. However, they are not the only criminal element that has to be taken into consideration. Evidence suggests that technology is increasingly seen as potential tool for terrorist organizations. This is leading to the emergence of a new threat in the form of 'cyber terrorists', who attack technological infrastructures such as the Internet in order to help further their cause. The paper discusses the problems posed by these groups and considers the nature of the responses necessary to preserve the future security of our society.

US launches cyber security plan

BBC says ,US President Barack Obama has announced plans for securing American computer networks against cyber attacks.

He said that from now on, America's digital infrastructure would be treated as a strategic national asset.

He announced the creation of a cyber security office in the White House, and said he would personally appoint a "cyber tsar".

Both US government and military bodies have reported repeated interference from hackers in recent years.

Security or Convenience

Another way the private sector can effect positive change is by embedding security into the products and services it brings to market. Sometimes natural market forces will drive these decisions, like built-in car alarms, insurance discounts for home security systems or embedded security tabs for DVDs and other media. Other times the government can legislate, regulate or litigate the change.

"If you buy a car, and get hurt because of a design flaw, the manufacturer has a strong safety liability in that case," says Ting-Peng

Liang, National Chair, Professor, and Dean of the College of Management at National Sun Yat-Sen University in Kaohsiung, Taiwan. "But if you get hacked because your system or software is poorly designed, the vendor has no security liability. You're left on your own to secure data and equipment you know nothing about."

When building security into products, however, companies must carefully consider the trade-offs consumers are willing to make against convenience or cost. GIO participants pointed out that Apple has been widely criticized for not including more security measures in its popular iPod music players. But a big

reason for the iPod's success has been its simplicity and ease of use, something that burdensome security requirements could undermine. Alternatively, participants pointed out the self-contradictory behavior of consumers who clamored for improved security features in Microsoft's Vista operating system, then complained incessantly about the same features upon release of the product.

"'How much security is enough?' is a question I grapple with every day," says Ingo Noka, Head, Visa Payment Security in Asia Pacific, Visa. "My biggest fear is that we are so concerned about security that we destroy the valuable things the Internet has to provide. I don't want the Internet to require consumers to hold three different security tokens to exchange information or make transactions, or require users to have to attain permission from multiple bodies just to post a simple comment on an online public forum. It will become like TV, which is not interactive. It's important to remember that the value of security is crucial in helping to build trust among users. You must be careful not to destroy that which you are trying to protect—in this case the interactivity and potential of the Internet."

PC SECURITY
IT TAKES 20 MINUTES FOR AN
UNPROTECTED PC TO GET INFECTED
WITH A VIRUS ON THE INTERNET.

IDENTITY THEFT
IN 2007, 127 MILLION
PERSONAL RECORDS WERE
LOST OR COMPROMISED.

HOME SECURITY
A HOME WITHOUT A SECURITY
SYSTEM IS TWO TO THREE TIMES
MORE LIKELY TO BE BURGLARIZED.

MOBILE SECURITY
83 PERCENT OF
WIRELESS OPERATORS
HAVE BEEN HIT BY
MOBILE DEVICE
INFECTIONS.

FLASH DISK SECURITY
10 PERCENT OF EMPLOYEES
REPORT FINDING A FLASH
DRIVE UNATTENDED IN A
PUBLIC PLACE.

AUTO SECURITY
CAR THIEVES STRIKE EVERY
26.4 SECONDS.

Security or Convenience

How can we enforce & adhere to the Cyber Law Obligations

Terms of use for Cyber Law Info (tm): Cyber Law, Entertainment Law, Intellectual Property Law & Litigation (v1.11)

1. Acceptance of terms of use and amendments

Each time you use or cause access to this web site, you agree to be bound by these terms of use, as amended from time to time with or without notice to you. In addition, if you are using a particular service hosted on or accessed via this web site, you will be subject to any rules or guidelines applicable to the said services, and they will be incorporated by reference within these terms of use. Please refer to this site's privacy policy, which is incorporated within these terms of use by reference.

2. The site editor's service

This web site and services provided to you on and through this web site are provided on an "AS IS" basis. You agree that the site editor exclusively reserves the right to modify or discontinue provision of this web site and its services, and to delete the data you provide, either temporarily or permanently; the site and may, at any time and without notice and any liability to you, The site editor shall have no responsibility or liability for the timeliness, deletion, failure to store, inaccuracy, or improper delivery of any data or information.

3. Your responsibilities and registration obligations

In order to use this web site or certain parts of it, you may be required to register a user account on this web site; in this case, you agree to provide truthful information when requested, and undertake that you are aged at least the thirteen (13) or more. By registering, you explicitly agree to this site's terms of use, including any amendments made by the site editor from time to time and available here.

4. Privacy policy.

Registration data and other personally-identifiable information that may be collected on this site is subject to the terms of the site's privacy policy.

5. Registration and password

You are responsible for maintaining the confidentiality of your password, and shall be responsible for all usage of your user account and/or user name, whether authorized or unauthorized by you. You agree to immediately notify the site editor of any unauthorized use or your user account, user name or password

6. Your conduct.

You agree that all information or data of any kind, whether text, software, code, music or sound, photographs or graphics, video or other materials ("content"), made available publicly or privately, shall be under the sole responsibility of the person providing the content or the person whose user account is used. You agree that this web site may expose you to content that may be objectionable or offensive. The site editor shall not be responsible to you in any way for the content that appears on this web site, nor for any error or omission.

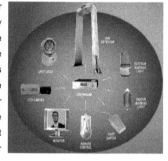

By using this web site or any service provided, you explicitly agree that you shall not:

(a) provide any content or conduct yourself in any way that may be construed as: unlawful; illegal; threatening; harmful; abusive; harassing; stalking; tortuous; defamatory; libelous; vulgar; obscene; offensive; objectionable; pornographic; designed to interfere or interrupt this web site or any service provided, infected with a virus or other destructive or deleterious programming routine; giving rise to civil or criminal liability; or in violation of an applicable local, national or international law;

July, 2009

(b) impersonate or misrepresent your association with any person or entity; forge or otherwise seek to conceal or misrepresent the origin of any content provided by you;

(c) collect or harvest any data about other users;

(d) provide or use this web site for the provision of any content or service in any commercial manner, or in any manner that would involve junk mail, spam, chain letters, pyramid schemes, or any other form of unauthorized advertising, without the site editor's prior written consent;

(e) provide any content that may give rise to civil or criminal liability of the site editor, or that may constitute or be considered a violation of any local, national or international law, including -- but not limited to -- laws relating to copyright, trademark, patent, or trade secrets.

7. Submission of content on this web site

By providing any content to this web site:

(a) you agree to grant the site editor a worldwide, royalty-free, perpetual, non-exclusive right and license (including any moral rights or other necessary rights.) to use, display, reproduce, modify, adapt, publish, distribute, perform, promote, archive, translate, and to create derivative works and compilations, in whole or in part. Such license will apply with respect to any form, media, technology already known or developed subsequently;

(b) you warrant and represent that you have all legal, moral, and other rights that may be necessary to grant us the license specified in this section 7;

(c) you acknowledge and agree that the site editor shall have the right (but not obligation), at the site editor's entire discretion, to refuse to publish, or to remove, or to block access to any content you provide, at any time and for any reason, with or without notice.

8. Third-party services

Goods and services of third parties may be advertised and/or made available on or through this web site. Representations made regarding products and services provided by third parties are governed by the policies and representations made by these third parties. The site editor shall not be liable for or responsible in any manner for any of your dealings or interaction with third parties.

9. Indemnification

You agree to indemnify and hold harmless the site editor and the site editor's subsidiaries, affiliates, related parties, officers, directors, employees, agents, independent contractors, advertisers, partners, and co-branders, from any claim or demand, including reasonable attorney's fees, that may be made by any third party, due to or arising out of your conduct or connection with this web site or service, your provision of content, your violation of these terms of use, or any other violation of the rights of another person or party.

this case, the site editor shall be relieved of any further obligation.

10. DISCLAIMER OF WARRANTIES

YOU UNDERSTAND AND AGREE THAT YOUR USE OF THIS WEB SITE AND ANY SERVICES OR CONTENT PROVIDED (THE "SERVICE") IS MADE AVAILABLE AND PROVIDED TO YOU AT YOUR OWN RISK. IT IS PROVIDED TO YOU "AS IS" AND THE SITE EDITOR EXPRESSLY DISCLAIMS ALL WARRANTIES OF ANY KIND, EITHER IMPLIED OR EXPRESS, INCLUDING BUT NOT LIMITED TO THE WARRANTIES OF MERCHANTABILITY, FITNESS FOR A PARTICULAR PURPOSE, AND NON-INFRINGEMENT.

THE SITE EDITOR MAKES NO WARRANTY, IMPLIED OR EXPRESS, THAT ANY PART OF THE SERVICE WILL BE UNINTERRUPTED, ERROR-FREE, VIRUS-FREE, TIMELY, SECURE, ACCURATE, RELIABLE, OR OF ANY QUALITY, NOR IS IT WARRANTED EITHER IMPLICITLY OR EXPRESSLY THAT ANY CONTENT IS SAFE IN ANY MANNER FOR DOWNLOAD. YOU UNDERSTAND AND AGREE THAT NEITHER THE SITE EDITOR NOR ANY PARTICIPANT IN THE SERVICE PROVIDES PROFESSIONAL ADVICE OF ANY KIND AND THAT USE OF ANY ADVICE OR ANY OTHER INFORMATION OBTAINED VIA THIS WEB SITE IS SOLELY AT YOUR OWN RISK, AND THAT THE SITE EDITOR MAY NOT BE HELD LIABLE IN ANY WAY.

Some jurisdictions may not allow disclaimers of implied warranties, and certain statements in the above disclaimer may not apply to you as regards implied warranties; the other terms and conditions remain enforceable notwithstanding.

11. LIMITATION OF LIABILITY

YOU EXPRESSLY UNDERSTAND AND AGREE THAT THE SITE EDTIOR SHALL NOT BE LIABLE FOR ANY DIRECT, INDIRECT, SPECIAL, INDICENTAL, CONSEQUENTIAL OR EXEMPLARY DAMAGES; THIS INCLUDES, BUT IS NOT LIMITED TO, DAMAGES FOR LOSS OF PROFITS, GOODWILL, USE, DATA OR OTHER INTANGIBLE LOSS (EVEN IF THE SITE EDITOR HAS BEEN ADVISED OF THE POSSIBILITY OF SUCH DAMAGES), RESULTING FROM OR ARISING OUT OF (I) THE USE OF OR THE INABILITY TO USE THE SERVICE, (II) THE COST OF OBTAINING SUBSTITUTE GOODS AND/OR SERVICES RESULTING FROM ANY TRANSACTION ENTERED INTO ON THROUGH THE SERVICE, (III) UNAUTHORIZED ACCESS TO OR ALTERATION OF YOUR DATA TRANSMISSIONS, (IV) STATEMENTS BY ANY THIRD PARTY OR CONDUCT OF ANY THIRD PARTY USING THE SERVICE, OR (V) ANY OTHER MATTER RELATING TO THE SERVICE.

In some jurisdictions, it is not permitted to limit liability and, therefore, such limitations may not apply in many cases.

12. Reservation of rights

The site editor reserves all of the site editor's rights, including but not limited to any and all copyrights, trademarks, patents, trade secrets, and any other proprietary right that the site editor may have for this web site, its content, and the goods and services that may be provided. The use of the site editor's rights. and property requires the site editor's prior written consent. By making services available to you, the site editor is not providing you with any implied or express licenses or rights, and you will have no rights. to make any commercial uses of this web site or service without the site editor's prior written consent.

13. Notification of copyright infringement

If you believe that your property has been used in any way that would be considered a copyright infringement or a violation of your intellectual property rights, the site editor's copyright agent may be contacted at the following address:

14. Applicable law

You agree that these terms of use and any dispute arising out of your use of this web site or the site editor's products or services shall be governed by and construed in accordance with local laws in force where the headquarters of the owner of this web site is located, without regard to its conflict of law provisions. By registering or using this web site and service, you consent and submit to the exclusive jurisdiction and venue of the location of the headquarters of the owner of this web site.

15. Miscellaneous information

(ID 1033 0 1) In the event that these terms of use conflict with any law under which any provision may be held invalid by a court with jurisdiction over the parties, such provision will be interpreted to reflect the original intentions of the parties in accordance with applicable law, and the remainder of these terms of use will remain valid and intact; (ii) The failure of either party to assert any right under these terms of use shall not be considered a waiver of that party's right, and that right will remain in full force and effect; (iii) You agree that, without regard to any statute or contrary law, that any claim or

July, 2009

cause arising out of this web site or its services must be filed within one (1) year after such claim or cause arose, or else the claim shall be forever barred; (iv) The site editor may assign the site editor\;s rights and obligations under these terms of use; in this case, the site editor shall be relieved of any further obligation.

How can we enforce & adhere to the Cyber Law Obligations

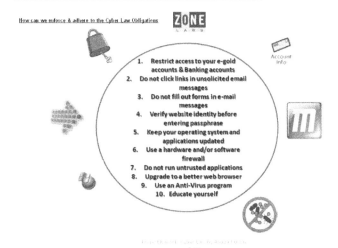

How can we enforce & adhere to the Cyber Law Obligations

1. Restrict access to your e-gold accounts & Banking accounts
2. Do not click links in unsolicited email messages
3. Do not fill out forms in e-mail messages
4. Verify website identity before entering passphrase
5. Keep your operating system and applications updated
6. Use a hardware and/or software firewall
7. Do not run untrusted applications
8. Upgrade to a better web browser
9. Use an Anti-Virus program
10. Educate yourself

Recommendations for a Secure Society

Biometrics

Biometrics refers to methods for uniquely recognizing humans based upon one or more intrinsic physical or behavioral traits. In information technology, in particular, biometrics is used as a form of identity access management and access control. It is also used to identify individuals in groups that are under surveillance.

Biometric characteristics can be divided in two main classes:

Physiological are related to the shape of the body. Examples include, but are not limited to fingerprint, face recognition, DNA, hand and palm geometry, iris recognition, which has largely replaced retina, and odor/scent.

Behavioral are related to the behavior of a person.

Examples include, but are not limited to typing rhythm, gait, and voice. Some researchers[1] have coined the term behaviometrics for this class of biometrics.

Strictly speaking, voice is also a physiological trait because every person has a different pitch, but voice recognition is mainly based on the study of the way a person speaks, commonly classified as behavioral.

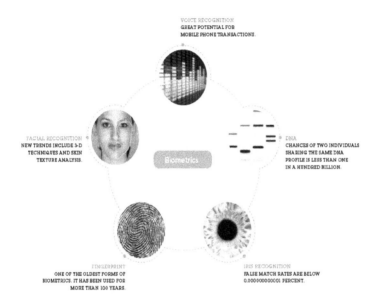

VOICE RECOGNITION
GREAT POTENTIAL FOR
MOBILE PHONE TRANSACTIONS.

FACIAL RECOGNITION
NEW TRENDS INCLUDE 3-D
TECHNIQUES AND SKIN
TEXTURE ANALYSIS.

Biometrics

DNA
CHANCES OF TWO INDIVIDUALS
SHARING THE SAME DNA
PROFILE IS LESS THAN ONE
IN A HUNDRED BILLION.

FINGERPRINT
ONE OF THE OLDEST FORMS OF
BIOMETRICS. IT HAS BEEN USED FOR
MORE THAN 100 YEARS.

IRIS RECOGNITION
FALSE MATCH RATES ARE BELOW
0.000000000001 PERCENT.

Use an effective antivirus solution that:

- Provides continuous, up-to-date, false network protection
- Detects malware and blocks spam at the gateway, or mail server
- Detects and deletes all viruses, worms, Trojans, identity thieves, etc.
- Blocks the spread of malware
- Institute an effective business security policy
- Conduct audits and actions on a regular basis
- Educate users staff through constant awareness programs
- Practice good account and password protocols
- Guard well unused ports
- Remove unused or illegitimate software
- Block web sites that affect productivity
- Set up remote access online threats to your organization's network to minimize intrusion.
- Use effective version control and configuration management tools to protect data
- Provide access control for employees regarding network requirements and also invoke limited access control
- Verify all vendors, contractors and third party suppliers

What can you do to protect your information and identity online?

(text illegible)

Cyber crime generally refers to criminal activity where a computer or network is the source, tool, target, or place of a crime. As the use of computers has grown, there is a new face to crime and this virtual modus operandi takes advantage of the internet to swindle people. For today's businesses, immediate access to information also means increased risks, such as phishing, identity theft, online fraud, etc.

Email scams and online frauds are quickly rising and it is therefore important that you take cautious steps to avoid such scams and fraudulent methods. The subject matter of most of these emails claim that you have won a prize of 1000s of dollars or may talk of amazing financial offers, guaranteed loans, investment opportunities, great discounts on products and so on.

Other steps you can take to keep your computer safe:

✓ Though email is a vital tool for most businesses, it can also be used as a mechanism to spread malware. Here are a few guidelines you can follow to further protect your business:

✓ Open email attachments from people that you know or known sources

✓ Never click onto a website link contained in an email, unless you can completely trust the sender of the message and the website that it is linking to

✓ Never respond to emails that appear to be from your bank requesting passwords

✓ Do not forward or respond to junk email, spam or "chain" emails – it wastes time and can make you a target

✓ Be very careful which websites you visit – certain websites can download malware without your knowledge

✓ Never install software from a website unless you can completely trust the vendor or provider

✓ Always check the website address (called a URL) and make sure that it is correct – some hackers will alter the URL very slightly and redirect you to a rogue site. When in doubt, do not proceed further.

✓ Today, any organization that is online is vulnerable to cyber threat; while adequate and timely protection can ensure successful business continuity.

Suggestions for better security

✓ Use strong passwords. Choose passwords that are difficult or impossible to guess. Give different passwords to all other accounts.

✓ Make regular back-up of critical data. Back-up must be made at least once in each day. Larger organizations should perform a full back-up weekly and incremental back-up every day. At least once in a month the back-up media should be verified.

✓ Use virus protection software. That means three things: having it on your computer in the first place, checking daily for new virus signature updates, and then actually scanning all the files on your computer periodically.

✓ Use a firewall as a gatekeeper between your computer and the Internet. Firewalls are usually software products. They are essential for those who keep their computers online through the popular DSL and cable modem connections but they are also valuable for those who still dial in.

✓ Do not keep computers online when not in use. Either shut them off or physically disconnect them from Internet connection.

✓ Do not open e-mail attachments from strangers, regardless of how enticing the subject line or attachment may be. Be suspicious of any unexpected e-mail attachment from someone you do know because it may have been sent without that person's knowledge from an infected machine.

✓ Regularly download security patches from your software vendors.

E - SECURITY TIPS

✓ **CHILDREN** : Do not give out identifying information such as Name, Home address, School Name or Telephone Number in a chat room. Do not send your photograph to anyone on the Net without first checking with your parents or guardians. Do not respond to messages or bulletin board items that are suggestive, obscene, belligerent or threatening. Never arrange a face-to-face meeting without telling parents or guardians. Remember that people online may not be who they seem to be.

✓ **PARENTS** : Use content filtering software's on your PC to protect children from pornography, gambling, hate speech, drugs and alcohol. There is also software to establish time controls for individual users (for example blocking usage after a particular time at night) and log surfing activities allowing parents to see which site the child has visited. Use this software to keep track of the activities of your children.

GENERAL INFORMATION

- ✓ Don't delete harmful communications (emails, chat logs, posts etc). These may help provide vital information about the identity of the person behind these.

- ✓ Try not to panic.

- ✓ If you feel any immediate physical danger of bodily harm, call your local police.

- ✓ Avoid getting into huge arguments online during chat or discussions with other users.

- ✓ Remember that all other internet users are strangers. You do not know who you are chatting with. So be careful and polite.

- ✓ Be extremely careful about how you share personal information about yourself online.

- ✓ Choose your chatting nickname carefully so as not to offend others.

- ✓ Do not share personal information in public spaces anywhere online, do not give it to strangers, including in e-mail or chat rooms. Do not use your real name or nickname as your screen name or user ID. Pick a name that is gender and age neutral. And do not post personal information as part of any user profile.

- ✓ Be extremely cautious about meeting online acquaintances in person. If you choose to meet, do so in a public place and take along a friend.

- ✓ Make sure that your ISP and Internet Relay Chat (IRC) network have an acceptable use policy that prohibits cyber-stalking. And if your network fails to respond to your complaints, consider switching to a provider that is more responsive to user complaints.

✓ If a situation online becomes hostile, log off or surf elsewhere. If a situation places you in fear, contact a local law enforcement agency.

✓ Save all communications for evidence. Do not edit or alter them in any way. Also, keep a record of your contacts with Internet System Administrators or Law Enforcement Officials.

GENERAL Définitions on Cyber

Cyber crime

Cyber crime encompasses any criminal act dealing with computers and networks (called hacking). Additionally, cyber crime also includes traditional crimes conducted through the Internet. For example; hate crimes, telemarketing and Internet fraud, identity theft, and credit card account thefts are considered to be cyber crimes when the illegal activities are committed through the use of a computer and the Internet.

Cyber forensics

computer forensics, is the application of scientifically proven methods to gather, process, interpret, and to use digital evidence to provide a conclusive description of cyber crime activities. Cyber forensics also includes the act of making digital data suitable for inclusion into a criminal investigation. Today cyber forensics is a term used in conjunction with law enforcement, and is offered as courses at many colleges and universities worldwide.

Cyber Monday

In retail and online shopping the Monday immediately following Thanksgiving (or the Monday immediately following Black Friday) in the United States is referred to as Cyber Monday. This is a busy day for online retailers as it was initially perceived as the day when employees would return to work and shop online for the items they did not purchase on the preceding Black Friday. The term Cyber Monday was first coined by Shop.org and first used in 2005.

cyberbullying

Slang term used to describe online harassment, which can be in the form of flames, comments made in chat rooms, the sending of offensive or cruel e-mail, or even harassing others by posting on blogs, Web pages or social networking sites (SNS) such as Facebook or MySpace. Unlike physical bullying, cyberbullying can often be difficult to track as the cyberbully — the person responsible for the acts of cyberbullying — can remain anonymous when threatening others online.

cyberjockey

A person who works online, usually as a volunteer, answering users questions and providing assistance to a new user (newbie) in online chat rooms and Internet discussion forums.

cyberlibel

Cyberlibel is a term used to describe defamation that takes place in cyberspace, meaning through the Internet. This includes false and damaging statements made about another person through e-mail, message boards, blogs, chatrooms, on Web sites, or any other Internet-based communication medium.

cyberloafing

Slang term used to describe employees who surf the net, write e-mail or other Internet-elated activities at work that are not related to their job. These activities are performed during periods of time when they are being paid by their employer. The individual is called a cyberloaf(er), while the act is cyberloafing. Same as cyberslacking.

Cybermediary

An individual or organization who retains a fee for negotiating or conducting transactions over the Internet as a third party, where the cybermediary does not take possession of or own the goods or services. Examples of a cybermediary include online insurance or real estate brokers.

cybernetics

Originally the study of biological and artificial control systems, cybernetics has evolved into many disparate areas of study, with research in many disciplines, including computer science, social philosophy and epistemology. In general, cybernetics is concerned with discovering what mechanisms control systems, and in particular, how systems regulate themselves.

The term was first coined by Norbert Weiner in 1943.

cyberprise

Slang term used to describe the merging of cyberspace and the enterprise.

The term cyberprise was first trademarked by the company Wall Data Inc., which used the word as its product name. Wall Data's Cyberprise is a suite of tools used for creating multiple online communities that include an enterprise's customers, vendors and partners. In 1999, Wall Data was acquired by NetManage, Inc.

cyberpunk

(1) A literary term used to describe a genre based on science fiction, but with emphasis on advanced technology. Cyberpunk was inspired by William Gibson's 1982 novel "Neuromancer".

(2) Slang term used to describe a lifestyle, or subculture based around technology such as computer games, online chatting, surfing, and other activities pertaining to the Internet and World Wide Web. It includes gamers, hackers, crackers, and phreaks.

cyberspace

(1) A metaphor for describing the non-physical terrain created by computer systems. Online systems, for example, create a cyberspace within which people can communicate with one another (via e-mail), do research, or simply window shop. Like physical space, cyberspace contains objects (files, mail messages, graphics, etc.) and different modes of transportation and delivery. Unlike real space, though, exploring cyberspace does not require any physical movement other than pressing keys on a keyboard or moving a mouse.

Some programs, particularly computer games, are designed to create a special cyberspace, one that resembles physical reality in some ways but defies it in others. In its extreme form, called virtual reality, users are presented with visual, auditory, and even tactile feedback that makes cyberspace feel real.The term was coined by author William Gibson in his sci-fi novel Neuromancer (1984).

cybersquatting

Cybersquatting is the act of registering a popular Internet address--usually a company name--with the intent of selling it to its rightful owner.

Comparing cybersquatting to online extortion, Senator Spencer Abraham, a Michigan Republican, has introduced to Congress the Anti-Cybersquatting Consumer Protection Act. This bill, if enacted, would make cybersquatting illegal. Violators would be charged a fine of up to $300,000.

The World Intellectual Property Organization (WIPO) has also outlined anti-cybersquatting tactics, which have been endorsed by ICANN (Ironically enough, someone recently registered www.wipo.com in order to sell it back to WIPO for several thousand dollars).Even though legislation has not been enacted, almost all cybersquatting court-case decisions are against cybersquatters.

Cyberveillance

A slang term normally used to describe the combination of hardware and software tools used for surveillance in the workplace. Cyberveillance is the monitoring of employee's computer activity. This refers to both on and off-line activity monitoring where managers are able to watch file changes on the system, the Web sites visited by the employee, instant messages, e-mails, and literally every keystroke made.

cyberpublisher

A slang term used to describe a person or group who publishes writing in digital format online on Web sites, PDF files, blogs and in other online spaces. May also be called cyberpublishing. Other industry-related cyber slang terms include cyberjournalist (a journalist who writes for online media) and cyberzine (an online magazine).

cyberbuck

A slang term used to describe money that is made through online channels. For example, the money a person might earn through affiliate programs.

cybernaut

A slang term used to describe a person who uses computers to communicate. It is said that this person — or cybernaut — travels in cyberspace. The word cybernaut is a play on the words "cyber" and "astronaut".

cyberculture

A slang term used to describe the emerging culture of those who are networked in cyberspace. It is a society of people who use computer networks for communication.

cyberlawyer

A slang term used to describe a lawyer who is an expert on the law as it relates to online communications. Other industry-related cyber words include cyberlaw and cyber forensics.

cybersuicide

Also called social suicide, cybersuicide is a slang term used to describe a suicide or suicide attempt that has been influenced by Web sites on the Internet. Cybersuicide is usually denoted by a public showing of the suicide or suicide attempt when the victim uses a Webcam to record the suicide attempt or provides a detailed discussion of their own suicide plans on public suicide-oriented Web sites and forums.

Bibliography, References

Cyber Scam & reporting

You can report with the Cyber Crime department if you have a case which is related to Cyber stalking, cyber harassment, Online harassment, unsolicited calls, pornographic MMS, online fraud, phishing, or even threat mails. You can also get professional assistance regarding any of the above crimes for free at the following in order to help online internet users.

Toll Free No.:- 1800 209 6789   SMS AGAPE to 54646

CFR2008a@consumerfraudreporting.org

FEDERAL TRADE COMMISSION

600 PENNSYLVANIA AVENUE NW

WASHINGTON DC 20580-0001

Phone: 1-877-FTC-HELP

 Working together for a safer London

Call the Met Police on 0300 123 1212

Address

Cyber Crime Police Station

COD Annexe Building Carlton House

1, Palace Road

Bangalore-560001 Telephone +91- 080- 2201026 +91- 080- 2943050

Fax +91- 080- 2387611 E-Mail ccps@kar.nic.in

Cyber Crime Police Stations in Different States of India

Location	Officer In Charge	Address	Telephone No	E-mail
Chennai	Sri Sudhakar	Assistant Comissioner of Police Cyber Crime Cell Commissioner office Campus Egmore, Chennai- 600008	55498211	cyberac@rediffmail.com baluac@vsnl.net

Chennai for Rest of Tamil Nadu	..S Balu	Cyber Crime Cell CB, CID Chennai	Mobile: 98410-13541 Off: 25393359	cbcyber@tn.nic.in Notification
Bangalore for the Whole of Karnataka	-	Cyber Crime Police Station C.O.D Headquarters, Carlton House, # 1, Palace Road, Bangalore - 560 001	22201026 22943050 22387611 (FAX)	ccps@kar.nic.in ccps@blr.vsnl.net.in http://www.cyberpolicebangalore.nic.in/ List of e-mail addresses of all Senior Police officers in Karnataka
Hyderabad	-	Crime Investigation Department, 3rd Floor, D.G.P. Office, Lakdikapool, Hyderabad-500004	23240663, 27852274 23297474 (Fax)	cidap@cidap.gov.in info@cidap.gov.in http://www.cidap.gov.in/cybercrimes.aspx
Mumbai	-	Cyber Crime Investigation Cell (Crime Branch, C.I.D), Annex-III Building, Police Commissioner Office, Crowford Market, Mumbai	22630829 22641261	officer@cybercellmumbai.com http://www.cybercellmumbai.com/
Lucknow		Cyber Crime Investigation Cell		www.cyberkeralam.in
Trivandrum		Cyber Crime Reporting Center	Call center (0471) 2727004	

Address of CBI Cyber Crime Cell

Supdt. of Police, Cyber Crime Investigation Cell Central Bureau of Investigation, 5th Floor, Block No.3, CGO Complex, Lodhi Road, New Delhi - 3, Phone: 4362203, 4392424 : EMail: cbiccic@bol.net.in : Web: http://cbi.nic.in/

Contact Address of Yahoo Mail and Hotmail Representative offices in India having responsibility as service providers for any Cyber Crime committed in India under ITA-2000 or other Laws.

Address of Yahoo India office:

Yahoo Web Services India Private Limited, 386 Veer Savarkar Marg, Opposite Siddhivinayak temple, Mumbai 400 025, 22 56622222, 22 56622244.e-mail: ad-sales-india@yahoo-inc.com

Address of MSN India Office:

MSN India, Prestige Takt, 23 Kasturba Gandhi Cross,Bangalore – 560 001, eMail: msnadin@microsoft.com, Tel: 91-80-2121212

- ✓ http://timesofindia.indiatimes.com

- ✓ http://www.dnaindia.com

- ✓ http://news.bbc.co.uk

- ✓ http://ibm.com

- ✓ http://en.wikipedia.org

- ✓ http://www.crime-research.org

- ✓ http://taosecurity.blogspot.com

- ✓ http://www.cyberpolicebangalore.nic.in

- ✓ www.usdoj.gov

- ✓ http://www.indlii.org

- ✓ http://www.nasscom.org

- ✓ http://pcquest.ciol.com

- ✓ Law enforcement

- ✓ www.cybercrime.gov

- ✓ U.S. Department of Justice Criminal Division Computer Crime and Intellectual Property Section.

- ✓ CERT® Coordination Center

- ✓ The first computer security incident response team.

- ✓ www.officer.com

- ✓ The world's most popular law enforcement web site. Professional Association Directory.

- ✓ Ahtcc.gov.au

- ✓ Australian High Tech Crime Centre.

- ✓ www.cpkn.ca

- ✓ Canadian Police Knowledge Network

- ✓ IFW - Internet Fraud

- ✓ Internet Fraud Watch.

- ✓ IFCC

- ✓ IFCC's mission is to address fraud committed over the Internet. For victims of Internet fraud, IFCC provides a convenient and easy-to-use reporting mechanism that alerts authorities of a suspected criminal or civil violation.

- ✓ Universities

- ✓ www.policy-traccc.gmu.edu

- ✓ The Transnational Crime and Corruption Center (TraCCC).

- ✓ www.cybercrimes.net
- ✓ The University of Dayton School of law.
- ✓ www.ojp.usdoj.gov/nij/
- ✓ The National Institute of Justice (NIJ).
- ✓ www.aic.gov.au
- ✓ Australian Institute of Criminology.
- ✓ www.cyber-rights.org
- ✓ Cyberlaw Research Unit, Centre for Criminal Justice Studies, University of Leeds, UK.
- ✓ Fletc.gov
- ✓ The Financial Fraud Institute (FFI).
- ✓ www.gocsi.com
- ✓ Computer Security Institute (CSI).
- ✓ www.thei3p.org
- ✓ The Institute of Information Infrastructure Protection (I3P).
- ✓ Asian School of Cyber Laws
- ✓ Asian School of Cyber Laws delivers education, training, consultancy and research in Cyberlaws, cybercrime investigation and cyber forensics.
- ✓ Nottingham Trent University
- ✓ Digital Forensics First Responder CPD.
- ✓ Forensics
- ✓ www.cops.org
- ✓ International Association of Computer Investigative Specialists.
- ✓ www.cpsr.org
- ✓ Computer Professionals for Social Diversity: Computer Crime Directory.
- ✓ www.ncfs.ucf.edu
- ✓ National Center for Forensic Science.
- ✓ www.investigation.com

- ✓ Kessler International - Forensic Accounting, Computer Forensics, Corporate Investigation.
- ✓ TeCrime International, Inc.
- ✓ High Technology Crime Investigation Computer Forensics & Digital Evidence.
- ✓ Forensics.ca
- ✓ The Forensics Science Portal
- ✓ Computer Forensics World
- ✓ Computer Forensics World is a vendor independent, interactive portal.
- ✓ Forensics Exams
- ✓ Forensicexams.org is a dynamic portal for computer forensic examiners to share information.
- ✓ Security
- ✓ www.securitydocs.com
- ✓ Directory of Security White Papers.
- ✓ www.oompusoccenter.com
- ✓ COMPUTER SECURITY CENTRE (csc).
- ✓ www.securitydocs.com
- ✓ Directory of Security White Papers.
- ✓ www.isalliance.org
- ✓ A Trusted and Reliable Public-Private Partnership for Information Sharing and E-Security Issues.
- ✓ Security installation news
- ✓ Info4Security provides the latest news, information and advice about security regulations, legislation, standards and reviews for Security Installers and Security management.
- ✓ Security Products Guide
- ✓ SourceSecurity.com is a definitive guide to the security industry featuring thousands of products, a comprehensive company directory and listing of major tradeshows and events.

- ✓ Legal
- ✓ mishpat.net
- ✓ Mishpat.Net - Internet Legal Information.
- ✓ portal.brint.com
- ✓ The Global Knowledge Network for Business, Information, Technology, and Knowledge Managers, Professionals, and Entrepreneurs.
- ✓ www.iipa.com
- ✓ The International Intellectual Property Alliance (IIPA).
- ✓ www.leeds.ac.uk
- ✓ The Department of Law at Leeds is recognised as one of the leading UK law schools.
- ✓ Globaldisaster.org
- ✓ Cyberterrorism Resource Center.
- ✓ Securities Fraud Class Action
- ✓ Fraud Lawsuit information. Contact a fraud lawyer for all your legal needs!
- ✓ Cybercrimelaw.net
- ✓ Cybercrimelaw.net is a presentation of penal laws on cybercrime around the world. The site currently contains information about the laws in 69 countries, including those preparing such legislation.
- ✓ Securities Attorneys
- ✓ Find securities attorneys or law firms specializing in securities litigation. Cases handled including securities fraud, internet securities fraud, stock fraud, bonds fraud, mutual funds fraud, investment fraud and churning scams.
- ✓ Other information resources
- ✓ Anti-Child Porn.org
- ✓ AntiChildPorn.Org (ACPO) is an organization, comprised of volunteers from all around the world, whose mission is to stop the sexual exploitation of the world's children.
- ✓ Fraud Aid
- ✓ Fraud recognition & prevention education, fraud victim advocacy, law enforcement support

- ✓ Cybercopmail.com
- ✓ The Home of Cybercop Internet Services.
- ✓ Homeof.org
- ✓ CyberSafe.US
- ✓ CriminalWatch
- ✓ Most Wanted Criminals, Crime Statistics, Sex Offenders, Terrorism.
- ✓ www.merchantfraudsquad.com
- ✓ The Worldwide E-Commerce Fraud Prevention Network.
- ✓ C4I.org
- ✓ Comprehensive portal offering computer security & intelligence information for governments, and corporations.
- ✓ ScamFraudAlert.com
- ✓ ScamFraudAlert - A Victim Forum A place where victims of scam or fraud can come and alert the public.
- ✓ Onguardonline.gov
- ✓ OnGuardOnline.gov - provides practical tips from the federal government and the technology industry to help you be on guard against Internet fraud, secure your computer, and protect your personal information.
- ✓ fraudwatchers.org
- ✓ FraudWatchers.org - Voluntary virtual organization dedicated to assistance, guidance, support and education regarding internet fraud, with a focus onto the advance fee fraud.
- ✓ Organisation For Safe Electronic Frontiers
- ✓ OFSEF mission is to establish a working relationship between the users, the service providers, and authorities in an effort to combat Cyber-Crime on national and ultimately a global basis.
- ✓ DIYSpy: your own investigation
- ✓ DIYSpy was formed to offer a unique reference point on conducting your own private investigations.
- ✓ Online Criminal Justice Degrees

✓ Resources about Criminal Justice for students.

Cyber View

Anti Virus

E-governance

Malware | E-mail

Law | Market

Password | Security

Salami attack

Act | Norms for Website

Threats

Internet Time Theft | Stalking

Mobile

Global Security | Cyber Space

Spam

Pornography | Trojan Attack

Outsourcing

Benefits | E-Security

Code of Conduct | Data Warehouse

Privacy | Logic Bomb

MIS

Software

Malware

Cyber ethics | Bank

Phishing

Data Diddling

Buffer overflow attack | Information Technology

www.ingramcontent.com/pod-product-compliance
Lightning Source LLC
Chambersburg PA
CBHW052148070326
40689CB00050B/2460